# The Curse
# of
# Louis Pasteur

## NANCY APPLETON, Ph.D.

ISBN 0-9672337-0-4

The information in this book is not intended as medical advice. Its intention is solely informational and educational. It is assumed that the reader will consult a medical or health professional should the need for one be warranted.

Printed in the United States of America

Choice Publishing
P.O. Box 3083, Santa Monica, CA 90403

# Table of Contents

# Acknowledgment

This book is dedicated to David Stein Ph.D., my primary faculty advisor at Walden University, where I wrote my Ph.D. dissertation on "An Alternative to the Germ Theory." Although David had some doubts at the beginning of my research, he supported me completely, gave me excellent advice, and helped me through some discouraging times. *The Curse of Louis Pasteur* brings those initial studies to fruition.

This book is also dedicated to all of you who are still looking for answers to your health problems. I hope you will find some answers to your questions in these pages.

# Introduction

# THE CURSE OF LOUIS PASTEUR?

## How Your Health Has Been Affected by It and What You Can Do About It

*Everything is a disease that makes man suffer.*
Roger Bacon (1214-1292)

When I finished my research and investigation into what causes disease, I realized I had no choice but to call this book *The Curse of Louis Pasteur*. In the late nineteenth century, Louis Pasteur's "germ theory" became the medical paradigm, the controlling medical idea, for the Western world. As you will see in these pages, in its simplest form, the germ theory proposes that the body is sterile and that germs from the air cause disease.

The paradigm of the germ theory has become a curse. In Pasteur's day—and ever since—other theories about the cause of disease have fallen on deaf ears because they have tended to contradict that paradigm. No matter how simple and logical an idea about disease may be, if it does not promote the concept of invasive germs and their specific cures, it does not "fit" into the medical paradigm.

More importantly, the germ theory is a curse because it has encouraged the individual to give up responsibility for dealing with his or her own health and to turn that responsibility over to the medical community. If germs cause disease, it stands to reason that our own health is beyond our control! Instead, that control belongs to the medical community, whose tireless researchers spend ever-increasing amounts of our money to find the right pill or potion to annihilate disease-causing germs.

This quest to cure disease through medication is at the heart of modern allopathic medicine ("conventional" medicine as we know it in the Western world) and the multi-billion dollar pharmaceutical industry. It is a quest that persists despite abundant evidence indicating that germs do not cause many of the illnesses that are so common in North America, including allergies, arthritis, osteoporosis, and others that fall into the category of chronic and degenerative diseases.

After more than a century of trying, the Pasteur paradigm has utterly failed in this quest. All major degenerative diseases are on the increase, as are infectious diseases. Every year, old symptoms are given new names — names like Herpes, AIDS, Epstein-Barr virus, Candida Albicans, environmental illness and fibromyalgia — to make them appear to be the work of new germs. Unless we turn this nonsense around, the list will only grow in the future.

It's true. Medicine has taken some of the pain and symptoms of sickness away. But people are still succumbing to disease at an increasing rate. They are living with pain and illness, and they are dying suffering of diseases they should never have developed in the first place. The ability to recover from degenerative disease does not lie in any magic bullet. It begins with identifying the cause and stopping it. If we want to find the cause of disease, we need to look at our twentieth-century lifestyle.

In the following chapters, I will show you how Pasteur's curse came about. Then you will see how that curse can be lifted if we heed the ignored, even rejected, discoveries of Pasteur's peers and scientists of the twentieth century. Finally, I will provide guidelines that will help you to regain responsibility for your own health and, in turn, regain and/or maintain optimal health.

If scientific experiments aren't your cup of tea, feel free to skim over the experiments I have described here to support my thesis. But there is other information here that is meant to be consumed slowly, especially those chapters about the consequences of the germ theory and the details of what you can do to improve your own health and, perhaps, that of your community. Remember, there is a glossary and index to help you when in need. If you would like more documentation, medical journals, and further information on the subjects covered, you will find a complete bibliography at the back of the book. It's all yours for the taking.

Until the medical community starts looking at causes rather than devoting its time to looking for cures, and until we start taking responsibility for our own health, I believe we are in trouble. I am hoping this fresh concept will bring new direction and diversified research into the medical community.

CHAPTER 1

# SOME STARTLING STATISTICS

*Physicians with the utmost of fame*
*Were called by when they came*
*They answered as they took their fees*
*There is no cure for this disease*

— Hilaire Belloc (1870-1953)

Have you ever wondered what really causes disease—not just infectious diseases like AIDS, but degenerative diseases like arthritis and heart disease? Have you ever puzzled over where germs come from? Do they just hover in the air? Are they lurking in some hidden place, waiting to attack us? Isn't it odd that some people will develop heart disease, others suffer from arthritis or cancer, and some remain disease-free? Why is it that many people will die during a plague, but some will survive? And what about AIDS? Why doesn't everyone who is exposed to the AIDS virus become HIV-positive? And why don't all who become HIV-positive develop full-blown AIDS?

This book will attempt to shed light on what causes disease and what you can do to enjoy a disease-free life. It will try to answer these questions so you will understand what causes symptoms such as headaches, joint pains, allergies, chronic fatigue, and falling asleep after meals.

## Who Gets Sick and Who Stays Healthy?

For more than one hundred years, Western medicine has been dominated by Louis Pasteur's germ theory. Pasteur believed that human blood is pure and sterile but can be contaminated by living, airborne pathogens (germs). He also believed that nothing changed form within the blood unless it was disturbed from outside by invaders such as germs.

According to Pasteur's theory, if your body is invaded by a germ (or a bacteria or virus), you will get sick. If you can manage to avoid germs, bacteria or viruses, you will stay healthy.

It's not that simple! Let's begin by imagining two colleagues, Suzanne and Bridget, who both work in sales jobs. They are both in their late forties, married with grown children, and are about the same height and build, with brown hair and dark eyes. Both are hard-working women who occasionally swap stories about their demanding sales managers.

Within the space of a week, both Bridget and Suzanne see their doctors because of overwhelming fatigue that does not go away, even with ten hours of sleep every night. Both women are losing weight, have no appetite, and are worried about losing their jobs because they are unable to concentrate. Both are diagnosed with a viral infection, the human immuno-deficiency virus (HIV).

This is where the differences begin. Within six months, Suzanne has had recurrent pneumonia, is plagued by yeast infections, and continues to lose weight. As with many AIDS patients, she is beginning treatment for cancer. Her physician, however, is not optimistic that the disease can be treated successfully. The diagnosis is that she will not live much longer than a few months.

In the same six months, Bridget has gained back some of the

weight she had lost. Fatigue is no longer a problem. She is back to sleeping six to seven hours a night and has become efficient at her job again.

Now let's take a different scenario, one that has nothing do with germs but everything to do with general health and well-being.

Imagine that both women are in car accidents and sustain the same injuries. Bridget heals rapidly and uneventfully and responds well to the medical care. Suzanne is not so lucky. She develops infections, is slow to heal, and has lingering side-effects that become a long-term problem. Weeks after Bridget is back at work, Suzanne is still struggling to get her strength back.

Why is this? What makes the difference in how two individuals respond to the same virus or to similar stresses to their health? Does it really have anything to do with luck?

Bridget heals rapidly because she has a strong immune system. What she eats, thinks, feels, and says, as well as other lifestyle habits such as exercise and stress reduction,that nourish her body systems, all contribute to her ability to repair tissue efficiently. Because her immune system and other body systems are healthy, her body is able to meet trauma, resist infection, stop and reverse degeneration, and heal itself.

A slow healer like Suzanne does not respond well to medical care. Her immune system has lost its healing power because of an unhealthy lifestyle that includes a poor diet, negative thinking, and inability to cope with stress. These unhealthy habits continually upset her body chemistry and make her body's systems less efficient.

What makes a difference between a sick person and a healthy one? The answer is quite simple. It is the efficiency of the body systems. It is the digestive system's efficiency at breaking down nutrients and turning them into fuel for the body. It is the immune system's ability to resist outside stressors and repair tissues. It is the vibrancy of the circulatory system, the glandular system, the nervous system and the respiratory system. When these systems are all functioning well, the body can adapt, adjust, resist, and live long and healthily, without symptoms. When these systems are not working properly, the body becomes a target for infectious, chronic, and degenerative diseases. These conditions flourish in a body with a weakened immune system and an inability to repair body tissues.

> The capacity to adapt to or to resist differently outside challenges is described variously as host resistance, tissue tolerance, constitution, resistance/susceptibility, predisposition, a healthy immune system, and homeostasis.

### Definitions:

*Bacteria* are usually one-celled organisms that live in the air, water, soil, animals, and plants. Many do not harm their hosts; others cause disease by producing poisons.

*Viruses* are smaller than bacteria, can only grow in living cells, and are capable of causing infectious diseases.

*Microorganisms (microbes)* are plants or animals too small to be seen by the naked eye. These bacteria, fungi, and protozoa may or may not cause disease.

*Germs* are any microorganism, especially one that causes disease.

*Pathogens* are any microorganisms capable of causing disease.

## We're Living Longer. So Why Aren't We Healthier?

It's true. We are living longer. The current life expectancy for an American man is 74.5 years; for the average American woman, it is 79.6 years. Many people are living into their seventies and eighties, but they certainly don't have healthy bodies! Diabetes, heart disease, cancer, osteoporosis, degenerative diseases of the nervous system, arthritis, allergies, chronic headaches, and environmental illnesses figure prominently in the lives of many elderly people, as well as in the lives of some middle-aged people.

Despite record billions spent on insurance and health care— more per capita than any other country in the world—the United States is far from the world's healthiest nation. Those life expectancy figures don't look as good when you look at them in relation to other countries. In a survey of nineteen industrialized nations, America ranked an unimpressive #15 for life expectancy. In that same group, the U.S. also rated #13 for public health spending.

Chronic diseases such as cancer, heart disease, diabetes, epilepsy, osteoporosis, migraine headaches, sinusitis, bronchitis, and allergies are all on the increase. Deaths caused by cancer alone increased from 193.8 per 1,000,000 in 1987 to 203.7 per 1,000,000 in 1992.[1] Every year, 798,000 new cases of diabetes are diagnosed in the U.S. In 1997, an estimated 15.7 million Americans were suffering from the disease—nearly 6 percent of the population![2] The death rate from diabetes has increased as well—from 15.4 deaths per 1,000,000 in 1987 to 19.1 deaths per 1,000,000 in 1992.[3]

According to Dr. Robert W. Pinner of the Center for Disease Control and Prevention, infectious disease increased 58 percent between 1980 and 1992. A study of death certificates revealed that for every 100,000 people, deaths from infectious diseases increased from 41 to 65. Once thought to be a thing of the past, infectious disease is now the third leading cause of death, after heart disease and cancer.[4]

And a number of new diseases that resist medical care have also emerged, including herpes, AIDS, Epstein-Barr virus, Candida Albicans, environmental illness, and fibromyalgia.

These are the latest disease statistics:

- One out of six of us will become diabetic.
- One out of three of us will develop cancer.
- One out of two of us will develop cardiovascular disease.
- One out of six couples will suffer from unexplained infertility.
- One out of seven women in the U.S. will develop breast cancer.

Among those nineteen industrialized nations, the U.S. is #1 in areas where nobody wants that distinction.

- The U.S. is #1 in percentage of infants born at low birthweight.
- The U.S. is #1 in the incidence of cancer among men.
- The U.S. is #1 in the incidence of breast cancer.
- The U.S. is #1 in coronary bypass operations per capita.
- The U.S. is tied with four other countries for #1 in infant mortality.

It's no coincidence that the U.S. is #1 in snack food consumption. It also has the dubious distinction of being in the top three in calorie consumption, the top four in fat consumption, and the bottom five in iron consumption.[5]

> Degenerative diseases are increasing, infectious diseases are on the rise, and one out of every six couples cannot give birth to a child. These statistics look as if we are killing ourselves off!

## How Did We Get Here?

America reached this undesirable position as a world leader because we are looking in the wrong place for the cause of disease. Inspired by Pasteur's idea that germs cause disease, the medical community embarked on its current aggressive search to discover the right weapons to destroy the microscopic villains.

Pasteur revolutionized the practice of medicine and surgery. His germ theory also spawned today's vast pharmaceutical industry, with its vaccines, antibiotics, painkillers, and a host of other medicines of all kinds. The germ theory became the medical paradigm of the twentieth century. It created the politics and economics of medical thinking and health. It also subtly shifted the responsibility for well-being away from the individual and onto the medical doctors. All these doctors needed to do was prescribe the right chemical, kill the offending microbe, and restore the body's sterility.

## You Don't Need to be Among Those Statistics!

While antibiotics and other medications may work miracles when the body is in crisis, the key to long-term good health does not lie in a magic, pharmaceutical bullet. I believe we do not need to live with symptoms or die with diseases. This book will explain some of the other theories about what causes disease. It will also show you how you can benefit from what you learn about these theories to take positive steps to eliminate your own health problems.

By the time you have finished reading, you will realize that you are responsible for your own health—you alone. A medical practitioner can relieve symptoms. There are substances that can help to detoxify the body of parasites, bacteria, viruses, fungi, and other unwanted invaders. Ultimately, however, you are the one who has to take charge. You are responsible for what goes into your mouth, what comes out of your mouth, as well as for what you think, feel, and do.

As the expression goes: "The monkey is on your back." In this book, I'll show you how to turn that monkey into a friend and ally. The explanation is simple and easy to follow. All the information comes from medical textbooks and peer-reviewed journals, publications that have already been scrutinized for accuracy. Because I believe that medical terminology must not be so complex that the average person can't understand it, I have used simple phrases whenever possible. I have also included a glossary of words that may be unfamiliar to you.

Let's get started.

CHAPTER 2

# GOOD HEALTH: A BALANCING ACT

*We must give up the idea that man's state of health will improve if more is done for him.*

Author Unknown

Recently I asked an acquaintance if he believed he was healthy. His immediate answer was, "Yes, of course." However, when I questioned him further, I found out he controls his high blood pressure with a prescription drug and takes antacids frequently for an upset stomach. Since his symptoms are controlled by medication, he thought he was in good health. I do not buy that idea for one minute. I believe he is deluding himself.

Our bodies either hum or honk, and this man's body is honking. His symptoms—high blood pressure and an upset stomach—are honks. The honks are telling him there's an obstacle on his path to good health.

## Your Body Hums — Balance

Good health is a continual feeling of well-being free of medication. It is an existence characterized by sound sleeping, refreshed awakening, and an absence of fatigue except after strenuous exercise. A person in good health has a minimum of symptoms such as allergies, drowsiness after meals, joint pains, gas, headaches, and so on.

The body that hums is a body in homeostasis - the balance that is key to optimal health.

## You're Honkings — Imbalance

Because of Pasteur's germ theory, we usually think of disease in terms of offending invaders, such as bacteria or viruses. But these invaders can't make any headway in a body that is merrily humming along. They can only cause disease if homeostasis is disrupted or disorderly.

When the homeostatic mechanisms are not working correctly, the body develops symptoms—it honks. It is unable to rejuvenate itself and heal readily. It can't stand up to the offending environmental agents that can cause disease, and it literally destroys itself, transforming its own healthy cells into diseased cells.

If we ignore our body's honks, we do so at our peril.

## Defining Good Health

Good health means that the body's systems are functioning optimally and are working in harmony with one another. The endocrine glands are secreting the right amount of their hormones. The digestive system is digesting food completely and allowing the nutrients to enter the cells so they can function properly. Blood is flowing freely through the circulatory system, taking with it plenty of oxygen and nutrients to all the cells. The immune system is removing unwanted particles easily, or is transforming them into substances the body can use.

If you are blessed to have all these systems working in full force, if you have no symptoms, go to bed happy, wake up happy, and know little fatigue, then your body is humming.

Headaches are never a problem. Arthritis, high blood pressure, psoriasis, indigestion, yeast infections, bloating, boils, canker sores, chronic fatigue—none of these troublesome symptoms play a role in your life. Your body's systems are all posed for health. Your body is in balance, in homeostasis.

Homeostasis has only one objective: to preserve the beneficial conditions of life in the internal environment. Every day we are bombarded with external influences that threaten that balanced internal environment. Some of these threats include becoming too hot or too cold, eating too much or eating foods that are not good for us, breathing polluted air, and being exposed to chemicals over a period of time.

Our cells, first singularly and then collectively as tissues and organs, can only survive when our bodies are strong enough to maintain homeostasis or to regain it quickly after we have been exposed to these environmental threats. If the homeostatic mechanisms are impaired, the body loses its resistance and becomes susceptible to disease, which may begin in a single tissue or system. The interdependence and close coordination of the many bodily functions, which work so well when we are healthy, may be upset by a chain reaction when any part of the system breaks down.

The normal state of health is not a static condition but a coordinated response of many systems and mechanisms. Fluctuations occur within a very narrow range. An imbalance of a point or two on the acid/alkaline scale (pH) is extremely disruptive to health. (See sidebar.) A few percentiles of variation of oxygen concentration in the blood can impair function. In the bloodstream, the slightest changes can be observed in the levels of cholesterol, calcium, urea nitrogen, and other chemistries. If the blood sugar content is continually elevated, the body chemistry becomes upset. (See sidebar.) An infinitesimal deficiency or excess of iron, copper, iodine, or any other mineral can cause a problem in the function of many body parts.

## Are You Humming or Honking?

I believe we do not need to live with symptoms or die with diseases. Now is a good time for you to assess your own health and take charge. Get out a pencil and answer these questions.

1. Do you have a hard time getting up in the morning?
2. Do you need more than seven hours of sleep at night?
3. Do you fall asleep after some meals?
4. Are headaches a problem for you?
5. Is it necessary for you to eat some form of sugar every day?
6. Do your joints hurt at times?
7. Is your skin a problem? Do you have acne, psoriasis, a rash, or eczema?
8. Does your stomach bloat?
9. Have you had more than one cold in the past year?
10. Is fatigue a constant in your life?
11. Do you sometimes have problems with either constipation or diarrhea?
12. Do your hands and ankles swell sometimes?
13. Do you have gas often?
14. Do you have indigestion?
15. Are there dark circles under your eyes?
16. Do you get canker sores?
17. Are yeast infections a problem?
18. Did you have a lot of cavities as a child?
19. Do you have mood swings?
20. Is there one food that you need to eat every day?
21. Are you on prescription medications?
22. Do you have asthma?
23. Do you sometimes have an irregular heartbeat?
24. Is there a food that you crave?

If you answered yes to more than four of these questions, there are parts of your lifestyle that could be upsetting your body chemistry and causing symptoms and disease. If they are not now causing problems, they may do so in the future. Read on to learn how you can keep your body in balance and take positive steps to eliminate your own health problems.

Our health depends on our ability to rise to the challenges of the external world. The first part includes those things in our environment that can be healthy or detrimental for the body. The air we breathe can be either fresh or polluted. The water we drink can be fresh and without chemicals or germs, or it can be polluted. Our food can be non-processed, free of pesticides, insecticides, and other chemicals, or it can contain numerous chemicals and have gone through many processes that our digestive system cannot handle. The construction materials, paint, carpets, microwave ovens, electrical systems, cleaning materials, heating and cooling systems we use in our homes, the cooking utensils, cosmetics, time we spend too close to a television or a computer—any one of these can compromise the body systems and homeostasis.

---

### The pH of the Body

The acidity/alkalinity of the body is another important factor. When the body is in homeostasis, the pH stays balanced in the bloodstream, saliva, urine and other parts of the body. When it is out of homeostasis, the body can become acidic or alkaline. Our body has buffer systems which use minerals—and can over-use minerals—to bring the pH back to homeostasis. To learn how to test and regulate pH, read page 191.

## Homeostasis and Blood Glucose Levels

There is increasing evidence that homeostasis, where a person is without symptoms and is in optimal health, is a much more narrow state than was previously recognized. One example of this is the blood glucose chemistry.

Most laboratories suggest the fasting blood glucose (the amount of glucose remaining in the bloodstream ten hours after eating) should be between 60 mg % and 110 mg %. However, research by Dr. Emanuel Cheraskin of the University of Alabama showed that individuals whose fasting blood glucose ranged between 75 mg % and 85 mg % had a minimum of gingivitis (periodontal disease) in their mouths.[1] The further their fasting blood glucose level was from 75 mg % and 85 mg %, the more likely they were to have gingivitis.

The second part of the external world deals with what we eat and what we think, say, and feel about that world. We have a choice in what we eat. Food can enhance or upset our body chemistry. So can our thoughts, feelings, and words. Our body chemistry can be upset without a word even being uttered. A negative thought or emotion can upset body chemistry. Exercise also plays a part in homeostasis. We have a choice to exercise or not. These are parts of the external world we can control, just as we can control many of the pollutants that surround us on a daily basis.

We can allow our twentieth-century lifestyle to upset our body chemistry, continually suppressing our immune system, or we can make changes that will enhance our body chemistry and our immune system.

> Dr. Cheraskin's research suggests that fasting blood glucose is a good indicator of homeostatic mechanisms in the body. Since blood glucose metabolism indicates how well we digest our carbohydrates (carbohydrate metabolism), this also plays an important role in homeostasis. [2]

We must keep our homeostatic mechanisms strong so that we can deal effectively with that world. If we are humming and homeostasis is orderly, life continues; if we are honking and homeostasis is continually being disrupted, our health is in jeopardy—disease may follow.

## The Truth about Sugar

By consuming a large amount of sugar over the years, many people have abused not only their blood glucose mechanism but also their insulin mechanism. When we eat simple sugars, our blood glucose goes up. The pancreas then responds by secreting insulin to bring the blood glucose back to homeostasis. Americans eat an average of 152 pounds of sugar per year. That is equivalent to over 1/2 cup every day! With this amount of sugar, our blood glucose and insulin mechanisms have to work continuously to regulate our blood sugar. The human body simply does not have the mechanisms to regulate the blood sugar levels and digest that vast amount of sugar.

There is also a correlation between blood glucose and weight. One researcher found that every 1 mg % increase in fasting blood glucose represented a corresponding average rise of 10 pounds of weight in both women and men weighing more than 99 lbs.[3] This is a strong indicator of the correlation between sugar, blood glucose, and obesity.

According to the Centers for Disease Control and Prevention, nearly 16 million Americans—6 percent of the population—have diabetes. This is the highest number of cases ever recorded. And unless we change our habits, that number will double in just one generation! Sugar certainly plays a part in this process. Read more, lots more, about the role that sugar plays in the degenerative disease process in my book, *Lick the Sugar Habit*.[4]

We are in control of much of our life, much more than many of us realize. Real health control, as well as the potential for full physical, mental, and emotional control, is built into the human being at birth. **The human body has its own innate intelligence.** When we allow it to, it will work subconsciously with its own natural computer—and it will hum rather than honk.

## Balancing Inputs with Outputs

Homeostasis is a bit like balancing the books in accounting. It is maintained by balancing inputs with outputs. An imbalance on either the input or output side of the equation can have a dramatic impact on health.

To take just one example, let's look at the body's enzymatic systems, of which there are thousands. Enzymes are substances that stimulate chemical changes in the body. There are two types of enzymes: metabolic and digestive. Metabolic enzymes help us to maintain good health in different parts of our body—in the eyes, liver, and circulatory system. Digestive enzymes help to break down food into its simplest form in the digestive tract. When the body is out of homeostasis, the metabolic and digestive enzymes cannot function optimally. They can't do the job they were meant to do.

In the case of digestive enzymes, this means that not all the food that is taken in can be digested. Some of this partially digested food gets into the bloodstream, where it plays havoc with a body that is doing its best to adapt. The immune system rallies to the defense to escort the unwelcome visitor out of the body. But the immune system can only respond properly for a time. It has other work to do. Its main job is to defend the body against outside assaults, not to deal with partially digested food particles. Using its defenses in this way puts a continual strain on the body that can exhaust the immune system and tax the endocrine and digestive systems, which work together in har-

mony. For more information on this subject rea
*Secrets of Natural Healing With Food.*

## The Feedback System

All the systems in the body have a feedback system, a slight, continuous push/pull that helps to maintain optimal balance. The feedback system consists of signals that are transmitted to different parts of the body and help to bring it back to balance when it has moved too far away from the center. One feedback mechanism is the body's ability to send signals to the controlling, conscious mind whenever homeostasis is threatened. The body then realizes it is hungry, thirsty, tired, in pain, or has other symptoms signaling that it doesn't feel right.

Another feedback mechanism involves the endocrine glands, which secrete hormones that help to regulate homeostasis. If one gland loses the ability to secrete enough of its hormone into the bloodstream, another gland will compensate by secreting more. This works well in a crisis situation, but it is not meant to be an ongoing response. It can have disastrous effects on the body if it continues over a period of time. (For more information on the Feedback System, see Chapter 6.)

## The Body's Ability to Adapt

Adaptation is a mechanism by which the body tries to preserve and maintain its health by adjusting to alterations in the conditions under which it functions.

If you cut yourself badly, for example, the body responds with a series of events designed to protect itself and ensure a supply of blood to the brain and the heart. The blood is made to clot faster. Bleeding slows the blood volume throughout the body. The peripheral blood vessels are constricted, reducing the flow in regions where loss of blood is most likely to occur. The cells of the body are adjusting to severe stresses and achieving altered states of equilibrium while preserving their state of health.

The large, bulging muscles of a laborer are another good illustration of cellular adaptation. Because of the heavy demand placed on the laborer's arms and legs, the individual muscle cells in these areas grow in size. They become larger because there are more of the tiny fibers that provide the compressed power of muscles. While a normal muscle cell would have 2,000 fibers, for example, the larger cell might have 4,000 fibers. The workload can now be divided among twice as many fibers, so no single muscle is overloaded.

The cells of the worker are completely normal. In fact, they're stronger than normal cells. They allow the laborer to do heavy work all day without excessive fatigue and with no injury to the cells. He can also meet emergencies, such as running from a fire or swimming through strong currents, challenges that would overwhelm someone who has not undergone such development.

Unfortunately, the body often adapts in ways that are not healthy. The liver's job is to filter chemicals that come into the body. When there is an increase in the level of chemicals the body is exposed to, the liver cells can respond by increasing their supply of enzymes. Over time, this can overload the liver.

How well we adapt in health and sickness is largely a function of the homeostatic mechanisms. The body's chemistry responds to such subtle changes that a negative thought, a food that does not digest, or eating too much food can be a problem for maintaining balance. Homeostasis can be upset by a change in a single pathway in the body's complex homeostatic network.

## Breaking the Chain Reaction

When one function of an organ or system breaks down, a chain reaction may occur. This is because the organs are so interdependent, cooperating beautifully when the body is healthy. The concept of holistic health implies that the entire body is involved in both health and disease. The homeostatic body—the body in balance—permits and encourages the proper performance of those internal functions necessary for growth, healing, and well-being. Among others, these functions include the regulation of mineral ratios, the production of enzymes, and the total digestive process.

"Most major chronic diseases probably result from the accumulation of environmental factors over time in genetically susceptible people," concluded an article in the *New England Journal of Medicine.* [5] I agree with this statement, but I would like to add a little more to it. Diseases do result from the accumulation of environmental factors such as poor diet, distress, and chemicals in our environment. Under these conditions, the body becomes overloaded, toxic, and is not able to maintain healthy homeostasis.

> In the long-term, I do not feel that any modality, whether it be in conventional or holistic medicine, will work until we look to see what we are doing to cause our own chronic or degenerative disease. The most important thing is to stop the cause. Find out what you are doing to cause your body to have symptoms and stop doing it. These symptoms could be diet-related, psychologically or spiritually related, chemical or drug-related, or they could be related to something in your environment. We all run to our pharmacy, a health food store, doctor, or health practitioner asking for a pill to fix our physical or mental problem. We hope that there will be some magic in the pill that will take our symptoms away. Sometimes magic pills can help, mostly to detox, but we must stop the cause. If we do not stop the cause and rely on pills, we are wasting our time.

In 1965, René Dubos, a medical historian and philosopher, pointed out that the body is imperfect in its attempts to adapt and maintain homeostasis. Homeostasis is only an ideal concept. The mechanisms involved in regulating homeostasis do not always return the body's functions to their original state. They can be misdirected. The body only has the ability to adapt to insults for so long. When it can no longer adapt, degeneration sets in. Health is the state that the body attains when an individual responds adaptively and restores the body to its original integrity.[6]

## Balance = Good Health
## An Ancient Concept

The term "homeostasis" was coined in the mid-1920s by the American physiologist Walter B. Cannon (For more on Cannon, see Chapter 6.) But he was building on a concept of balance that dated back to ancient Western, Eastern and Middle Eastern civilizations.

The balance = good health equation was first suggested by Hippocrates (c.460 BC-375 BC) and the ancient Greeks. Often referred to as the "Father of Medicine," Hippocrates considered health to be a state of harmonious balance and disease a state of disharmony.[7] He and his contemporaries believed that harmony and balance existed between organs, between body fluids, and between body and soul. When the body was out of harmony and balance, illness occurred.

Hippocrates studied the entire patient in his environment, noting the effects of climate, food and occupation on health. "Our natures are the physicians of our diseases," he said, describing the healing forces we all have within us as the "healing power of Nature." It was the physician's objective to restore harmony with food, exercise, or rest, and with medicinal remedies designed to remove the harmful excesses. This conservative approach was designed to let nature do the healing and, above all, not to cause harm.[8]

The Greeks' ideas on equilibrium and health evolved further under the philosopher Aristotle (384 BC-322 BC). He felt that a healthy body worked through what he described as a "homeostat," a device that returned the body to a state of equilibrium even when it was subjected to stimuli that disturbed this balance. Everything was tied to this state of equilibrium, including the psyche and emotions, and nothing could be regarded as a separate component.[9]

To lead a healthy life, Aristotle believed, the condition of balance had to be maintained. This could only be achieved if the body had an adequate feedback system, a means by which signals were transmitted to different parts of the body to help to move it back into balance when it moved too far off center.

This psychological viewpoint was shared by another philosopher, Epicurus (341 BC-270 BC). In his writings, he referred to psychological stress and suggested that an individual's quality of life could be improved by coping with what we would now describe as emotional stressors.[10]

## Eastern Perspectives on Balance

As early as about 120 AD in India, Eastern philosophers had reached similar ideas about the importance of balance in health. A general medical textbook from that time, the *Caraka*, described health as a balance of bodily elements known as *dhatus* and a happy mental state called *prasana*. When disturbance of this equilibrium brought on illness, the healer was forced to investigate what was causing the problem. Illness-producing factors included imbalances of three internal waste products or *doshas:* wind, bile, and phlegm. The goal of Hindu medicine was holistic. It sought to restore the balance of the *tri-doshas* and *dhatus* through diet and vegetable drugs, and to eliminate the mental anguish accompanying illness.

The Middle Eastern approach incorporated the Hindu teachings with the Grœco-Roman medical doctrine. According to both religious and philosophical ideas, Islamic healing involved both body and soul. Health could only be achieved through harmony with the entire cosmos.[11]

# Coming Back Full Circle

Over one thousand years later, during the Middle Ages, good health was still linked to this notion of a balanced physical, emotional, and spiritual state. To help people achieve this state, European hospitals were set up by religious orders and attached to abbeys, monasteries, and convents. Doctors prescribed diet, rest, sleep, exercise, and baths. When necessary, they would also administer purgatives or "bleed" patients.[12]

These ideas of balance were some distance from those of primitive societies that ascribed illness to the supernatural powers they believed governed their lives. Primitive peoples saw disease as an entity unto itself, a potent demon that attacked, penetrated, struggled to dominate, and possibly even killed its unfortunate host. Offend the gods, an ancestor, or an evil witch and you would be struck down as punishment. Lead a sinful life and you were tempting fate.

Of course, this primitive idea about disease is no longer widely believed, which makes it all the more ironic that Pasteur's germ theory, based on a similar concept of invading attackers, has such a strangle-hold on twentieth century medicine. As medical writer Alberto Seguin described in an article entitled "The Concept of Disease," the demonic idea of disease reached its full height with the germ theory. It became possible to bring together rational and scientific thought with the irrational tendency to personalize disease. The germ is the scientific form of the demon that attacks and kills.[13]

# Conclusions

Let's go back to the beginning of this chapter, to my acquaintance with the upset stomach and high blood pressure. If we consider his symptoms in the light of what we have learned about homeostasis, then it becomes clear that his body is out of balance—but correcting that imbalance is within his control. If we follow the principles behind the germ theory, his body is honking because of a specific factor, something beyond his control. Rather than looking at what he is doing to cause the symptoms, he relies on his doctor and on over-the-counter or prescription medications to stop the honking.

The germ theory may have revolutionized the practice of medicine, but it also moved us away from an understanding based on centuries of observation: balance and good health are inseparable. In the next chapter, we'll see how Pasteur developed his germ theory and why it has had such an enormous impact on medicine.

CHAPTER 3

# LOUIS PASTEUR AND THE GERM THEORY OF DISEASE

*If a man has committed himself to the pursuit of theoretical science, he should never, for the sake of his peace of mind and the success of his investigations, let himself be lured into the practical application of science.*

— Louis Pasteur (1822-95)[1]

L ouis Pasteur was a man with a mission. Vocal and flam-boyant by nature, he was a spectacularly successful pro-moter of his own views. He was a prolific writer, widely published in the science publications of his time, and he had the zeal to preach his gospel to the world.

At first a teacher in secondary schools and at universities, Pasteur eventually became Director of Scientific Studies at the École Normale Supérieure at the Sorbonne in Paris. In 1862, he was admitted into France's prestigious Academy of Science. Five years later, fortune shone on Pasteur again when Emperor Napoleon III, an admirer of his work, created a laboratory of physiological chemistry for him at the Sorbonne. This allowed him to move out of his position as Director, a job that wasn't quite to his liking.

Philosophically speaking, Pasteur had an ally in Napoleon III, who came to power in 1852. The Emperor believed in a police state and in using complete control to rule. Pasteur's mechanistic idea of disease, finding the right cure for each germ, fit into this philosophy of control. **Giving the responsibility to the state to cure disease is control. It takes responsibility—and power—away from the individual.**

## The Origins of the Germ Theory

Pasteur's germ theory arose from the cellular theory set forth in 1839 by Matthias Schleiden and Theodor Schwann. The cellular theory is the universal principle of development for the elementary parts of organisms. It states that cells make up tissues, tissues make up organs, organs make up systems, and systems make up the human organism. The specialized disciplines of embryology, cellular pathology, cellular physiology, and immunology have all originated from this theory.[2]

Other cells of a simpler nature, called bacteria or viruses, can attack, subsist upon, and destroy the more complex organism, whether it is plant or animal.[3]

From this comes the theory that external, preexisting microbes invade the human body and cause disease.

While a variety of scientists initiated the germ theory, it was Schleiden and Schwann, and then Jakob Henle, Louis Pasteur, and Robert Koch who helped bring it to its maturity. And it was Pasteur who received the lion's share of the credit.

Another extension of the cellular theory is the doctrine that states that disease is caused by a specific factor—a bacterium, a virus, or a hormonal deficiency. This mechanistic viewpoint pinpoints a single cause of disease and forms the basis of modern medicine. It does not deal with the body as a whole. It gained popularity because it made disease simple to understand.

If a single factor isolated in an experimental animal could be the cause of disease, then a mechanical procedure or substance could be effective in treating it.[4]

How did Pasteur develop this mechanistic view of the cause of disease? And what led him to the famous (or infamous) theory of disease that has so strongly influenced our idea of illness and the direction of modern medicine?

## Fermentation

Some of Pasteur's early research involved fermentation, the biochemical process by which organic substances, particularly carbohydrates, are decomposed and split into more simple compounds. The rising of bread dough, the souring of milk, and the conversion of sugars and starches into alcohol all involve the fermentation process. Fermentation is always initiated by enzymes in the cells of living organisms. An enzyme is a natural catalyst that brings about a chemical change without being affected by it. Many industrial chemicals and a number of antibiotics used in modern medicine are produced by fermentation under controlled conditions.

One of Pasteur's challenges in those early experiments was a problem that had perplexed France's winemakers for years: they had been trying to keep their wines free of diseases that made them turn sour and bitter. This unpalatable wine was not only a concern for the wine-drinking French; it was also a business problem. It set limits on the country's wine exports, because the winemakers often had to worry that their wine would be spoiled when it reached its destination. If they could prevent this spoilage, then the French wine industry would grow as they felt it should.

When Pasteur examined the diseased wine under a microscope, he saw the yeast plants used in the fermentation process. While certain types of yeast produced good wine, others could cause the wine to become sour. But along with the yeast that starts healthy fermentation, he also saw other microscopic organisms. He believed these microorganisms entered from the air.

This research led Pasteur to say that fermentation depended upon the activity of living microorganisms.[5] He showed the winemakers that, by heating their wine to a certain temperature, they could kill unhealthy ferments without hurting the flavor of the wine. Thus, the word "pasteurization" was coined.[6]

## Research on Milk

Pasteur then turned his attention to the souring of milk. He discovered that little gray patches formed on the sides and bottom of vessels that contained milk. Using a microscope, he saw that the gray patches were made up of tiny globules much smaller than those of yeast. He reasoned that this gray material might be connected to the ferment of milk. The ferments in the alcohol and the milk belong to a group of plants called bacteria.[7] "Fermentation," he wrote, "is the consequence of a development of vegetable cells the germs of which do not exist in the saccharine juices within fruits."[8]

As a result of his investigations with the wine and milk, Pasteur reached the following conclusions:

- each kind of fermentation was due to a specific kind of outside organism;
- each kind of organism needed a particular set of environmental conditions for its growth and reproduction;[9]
- when an organic medium is adequately sterilized and protected from outside contamination, germs will not appear;
- microorganisms living everywhere in nature cause fermentation, decomposition, and putrefaction;
- these microorganisms do not develop from the decomposing or fermenting fluid but come into it from the outside;

- when sterile liquid is exposed to sterile air, it will remain sterile.[10]

Pasteur believed that the germs of microscopic organisms abound on the surface of all objects, in the air and in water. Wines, beer, and vinegar undergo none of their usual changes in pure air; nor do blood, urine, and other body fluids.[11] He also believed that the tissues of normal, healthy animals are bacteriologically sterile and that bacteria are not normally found within the body proper. It was the presence of bacteria in the body, he said, that caused cells to decompose, or putrefy.[12]

Science has since proven Pasteur wrong on this subject. Bacteriologists have found that all animals need healthy bacteria in their bodies in order to live. In fact, animals delivered by Caesarian section in aseptic (germ-free) conditions, kept in aseptic cages, and fed sterile food and water do not live more than a few days. It would seem that this "contamination" by exogenous bacteria (bacteria from outside) is essential for healthy life.[13]

## What Causes Fermentation?

The scientific community had been puzzling over this question for years before Pasteur began working in this area. 'If microbial action causes the souring of milk, alcoholic fermentation of sugar beet juice, the conversion of grape juice into wine, the conversion of wine into vinegar, the putrefaction of meat and many other changes that take place in organic matter,' they wondered, 'where did the microorganisms responsible for these changes originate? Did they originate each time anew in the product, or did they already exist somewhere, ready to start their activities when conditions were right for them? Did yeast and other ferments by-products cause fermentation? Or were they the by-products themselves?'[14]

Pasteur reasoned that if tiny living organisms were responsible for diseases in wines, the same exterior germ could be responsible for disease in animals and human beings. The germ theory was founded on this assumption that disease was an entity that could be overcome and eliminated. When he gave his acceptance speech to the French Academy of Science, Pasteur pointed out that the experimenter was one who tried continually to conquer nature. He felt that, through experimentation, he could conquer nature and change its laws.[15]

## The Question of Spontaneous Generation

As far as the French Academy of Science was concerned, the question was not only where do germs come from, but might they begin with spontaneous generation? Simply put, the doctrine of spontaneous generation states that living organisms can arise from either inorganic matter (abiogenesis) or organic matter (heterogenesis).[16] Early in his career, Pasteur had researched spontaneous generation using the abiogenetic method. He tried to create life artificially by means of chemical and physical forces. After many unsuccessful attempts, he put this idea to rest.

Another French scientist Félix Archimède Pouchet (1800-1870) spent most of his life researching spontaneous generation using the heterogenetic method. In 1859, Pouchet wrote *Heterogenesis: a Treatise on Spontaneous Generation,* in which he presented experimental, embryological, philosophical, and theological evidence in favor of spontaneous generation.[17] According to this theory, new organisms develop from the effects of a mysterious *force plastique.* This force can be found only in living organisms or in plant and animal debris. It is not found in inorganic matter.[18] In a paper he offered to the Academy of Sciences, Pouchet described the appearance of microorganisms in boiled hay infusions. He steeped the hay in water to extract its soluble parts and sterilize it, then exposed the hay infusion to artificially produced sterile air or oxygen. Germs appeared. From this development, he attempted to prove his theory of spontaneous generation, stating that "the life force has been passed on successively through an uninterrupted chain of being since creation."[19]

Pouchet denied abiogenesis, since he believed that only "organic molecules" were endowed with the *force plastique*. For organic molecules, it seemed to him, "there is no death, only a transition to a new life."[20] (This concept of transition of matter to a new life is an entirely different way of viewing matter, which will be explored later in the book.)

When Pouchet approached Pasteur with this information, the latter is said to have replied: "The experiments I have made on this subject are too few and, I am obliged to say, too inconsistent in results . . . for me to have an opinion worth communicating to you."[21] This seems to have been a way for Pasteur to disregard Pouchet.

In 1862, the French Academy of Sciences added fuel to the fire by setting up a contest to prove or disprove spontaneous generation. Of the various scientists who entered the competition, Pouchet and Pasteur were the most prominent. But the commission appointed by the Academy to judge the experiments was hardly unbiased. It was made up of men who favored Pasteur and who declared themselves opponents of spontaneous generation from the outset.

When the commission announced it had selected Pasteur before the members had even read Pouchet's research paper, Pouchet withdrew his entry. Pasteur received the prize uncontested on the basis of his 1861 essay, "Ideas about Organized Cells that Live in the Atmosphere." He maintained there was nothing in the air, no mysterious principle, no gas, no fluid, no ozone, no other medium, that was capable of arousing life in an infusion or any substance.[22]

Another contest was held. More experiments were carried out. But the judges were no more sympathetic to Pouchet. The Academy observed Pasteur's experiments and once again supported his claims. In the report that ended the spontaneous generation controversy in France, the commission did not veil its contempt for Pouchet and his colleagues.[23]

Although Pasteur had spoken often of the value of the "experimental method," he and the commission had violated one of its fundamental concepts. To comply with the experimental method, Pasteur would have had to redo Pouchet's experiments and find them false. Historian John Farley summed up the violation by saying:

> This violation is even more remarkable in the case of spontaneous generation since, logically speaking, opponents of the doctrine, being unable to prove that no organisms arise spontaneously, could do no more than falsify those experiments said to prove its occurrence. As Pasteur recognized often, in the observational sciences, unlike mathematics, the absolute, rigorous demonstration of a negation is impossible.[24]

Pasteur never conducted an experiment that could prove spontaneous generation did not occur.[25] Since the germ theory is based on the idea that spontaneous generation does not exist, it suited him well not to do any experiments that might prove otherwise. "It is the power of man to make parasitic maladies disappear from the face of the globe," said Pasteur, "if the doctrine of spontaneous generation is wrong, as I am sure it is."[26]

Pasteur later conceded it was impossible, in principle, to give a totally conclusive experimental proof in favor of or against spontaneous generation.[27] After reconsidering the matter, he said:

> In the present state of science, it is impossible to prove that there can be no self-creation of life apart from the pre-existence of similar living forms.[28]

> . . . I have looked for it [spontaneous generation] for twenty years without discovering it. No, I do not judge it impossible.[29]

Throughout the controversy, Pasteur admitted that his own repeated attempts to prevent the appearance of microbial life in infusions succeeded only rarely, perhaps less than 10 percent of the time. Yet, rather than admit the bacteria had originated spontaneously, Pasteur refused to admit the experimental evidence and continued to look for an alternate explanation. "I did not publish these experiments," he wrote, "for the consequences it was necessary to draw from them were too grave for me not to suspect some hidden cause of error in spite of the care I had taken to make them irreproachable."[30]

Although Pasteur did not specify the grave consequences he feared, historians John Farley and Gerald Geison believe that spontaneous generation must have been one of them.[31]

Pasteur defined as "unsuccessful" any experiments, including his own, in which life mysteriously appeared. Any experiments that produced an opposite result, he considered to be "successful."

## Another Side of Louis Pasteur

One of Pasteur's biographers, René Dubos, wrote many articles and three glowing books on Pasteur.[32] The first of these books, *Louis Pasteur – Free Lance of Science*, which Dubos wrote in 1950, is a fairly straightforward accounting of Pasteur's research and discoveries. Ten years later, toward the end of his second book, *Pasteur and Modern Science*, Dubos departed from the usual direction of Pasteur's biographers and added a few paragraphs about other factors, apart from the germ theory, that are involved in the control of disease. As Dubos wrote, "The hereditary constitution of the patient, his nutritional state, his emotional equilibrium, the season of the year and the climate are among the factors that can affect the course of infection." Dubos believed that Pasteur understood all of these factors. He went on to say that if Pasteur had been alive in 1960, he would have been very much disturbed that his followers had emphasized the germ theory to the exclusion of his other work.[33]

In 1976, *Louis Pasteur – Free Lance of Science* was re-released in a new edition with added information. Two new chapters explain that Pasteur understood how important the environment and an individual's own immune system were to fighting disease. In his later books, Dubos refers many times to Pasteur's ideas on the immune system, although there is no documented evidence to support them.[34] He believed Pasteur's ideas on the immune system represented the scientist's undeveloped genius side, a side that Dubos felt "might be more important in the long run."[35]

While a great deal has been written about Pasteur, none of his biographers explores this side or addresses the issue of the environment, the immune system or the terrain.[36] Émile Duclaux, Pasteur's research assistant and biographer, wrote about the capacity to resist disease, but in terms that place little responsibility on the individual. According to Duclaux, Pasteur believed that "the resistance of each living being . . . is a question of species, a question of individual place and time, the quantity of the germ or inoculating material, and the temperature."[37]

Since Dubos was a biochemist and bacteriologist, perhaps he came to his own conclusion that the individual was far more responsible for his health than Pasteur believed. Perhaps he wanted to put Pasteur in his own camp. Or maybe Dubos became concerned about the way medicine was going and wanted to try to change it. Pasteur's influence with the germ theory was vast. There seemed to be no turning back, particularly during the first half of the twentieth century. Even today, the path seems "Pasteurean." We continue to look for magic pills and potions rather than to the individual's lifestyle.

## New Research into Pasteur's Science

Over the past century, Pasteur's friends as well as his critics have questioned his scientific methods and his character. Even

Duclaux, Dubos, and others who wrote favorably about Pasteur expressed doubts about his scientific integrity. John Farley, Gerald Geison, E. Douglas Hume, Imago Galdston, and others have developed such doubts into strong criticisms. There has been considerable controversy over who developed the germ theory first,[38] who first discovered that the silkworm disease was a parasitical disease,[39] and whether spontaneous generation was still an issue in spite of Pasteur's research.[40]

The most recent and best-documented information about Pasteur comes from Gerald L. Geison, a Princeton history professor and leading Pasteur scholar. In a lecture before the American Association for the Advancement of Science, Geison described Pasteur as "by no means always humble, selfless, ethically superior . . . quite the opposite."[41] Geison is also quoted as saying that he found Pasteur's "behavior and conduct in general unlikable through much of his career. He [was] not a very appealing human being."[42]

Until twenty years ago, much of Pasteur's scientific work lay buried in elaborate notebooks and other private documents, a vast collection of thirty bound volumes of unpublished correspondence, lecture notes, school records, and more than 100 laboratory notebooks. These notebooks amount to perhaps 10,000 pages covering Pasteur's forty-year scientific career. At his request, all of the papers had been kept private and remained in his family. They did not become public until the late 1970s, eighty years after his death, when his last surviving male heir, a grandson, gave the entire collection to the Bibliothèque Nationale (France's National Library) in Paris.

Geison traveled to Paris to study Pasteur's papers and spent more than a year learning to read the scientist's pinched handwriting.[43] He found questionable scientific conduct in a series of Pasteur's studies on anthrax, a disease of farm animals that can be transmitted to humans. In one article, Pasteur announced he could produce a new vaccine by exposing the deadly anthrax organism to oxygen to reduce its strength. The vaccine was successful in a public demonstration to protect fifty sheep from infectious disease. Pasteur then "basked in applause" from officials and reporters in the French village of Pouilly-le-Fort. According to a footnote in one of his lab notebooks, however, Pasteur had used another vaccine approach in which he weakened the anthrax with chemicals rather than exposing it to oxygen. An obscure veterinarian by the name of Jean-Joseph Henri Toussaint developed the chemically treated vaccine first and had visited Pasteur's laboratory to discuss it.[44]

"Pasteur deliberately deceived the public and scientific community about the precise nature of the vaccine he used," said Geison, calling it a "clear case of scientific misconduct. . . . He knew full well he was lying."[45] Soon after, Pasteur made available his own oxygen-attenuated approach, and it became the preferred method. As for Toussaint, he suffered a nervous breakdown and died shortly afterwards.[46]

Another example of questionable conduct involved the first use of the rabies vaccine in humans. Joseph Meister, a nine-year-old French peasant, arrived unannounced at Pasteur's door, having been bitten fourteen times by a dog that was thought to have rabies. Pasteur administered his new rabies vaccine to the boy. He then published a paper reporting that he had tested the vaccine on fifty dogs without a single failure before he used it to treat young Meister. In his studies of the notebooks, Geison discovered Pasteur had extensively tested a vaccine on dogs, but the approach he used to test was exactly the reverse of the one used on Meister. Pasteur gave the boy injections of successively stronger doses of a rabies virus. He had no conclusive animal or human results to show that the technique worked or that the vaccine played a part in saving the boy's life.[47] A medical colleague, Émile Roux, had refused to participate in the Meister rabies trial on the grounds it was "an unethical form of human experimentation."[48] But none of this sullied Pasteur's reputation in the eyes of his biographers.

# Conclusions

Pasteur's germ theory implies that humans have little control over invasive microbes, unless they can find the right medicine to kill them. Government and pharmaceutical companies fund crusade after crusade to kill the foreign invader: the germ.

From the germ theory came pasteurization (killing the germs, along with many valuable enzymes), and now ultra-pasteurization (which kills all of the enzymes), antibiotics, antiseptics, and vaccines. These scientific advancements are all in pursuit of killing the germ or discovering the right cure for the common cold and other diseases.

Although Pasteur's basic research was on the germ theory, he may have had some understanding of the role that the body plays in disease. For unknown reasons, he chose to pursue the former path. Other scientists, some of them working at the same time as Pasteur, not only understood the body's role in the disease process but chose to devote their lives to this study. The next chapter introduces the work of one of them: Claude Bernard.

CHAPTER 4

# CLAUDE BERNARD AND THE INTERIOR ENVIRONMENT

> *What we already know is a great hindrance into discovering the unknown.*
>> Claude Bernard (1813-1878)[1]

C laude Bernard had an unconventional background for a scientist. As a young boy growing up in a small village in France, Bernard's first love was writing, and his efforts were rewarded with success. A vaudeville comedy he wrote, *La Rose du Rhône* was so well-received in his home town that he was inspired to follow his dream to Paris in the hopes of becoming a famous playwright.

It was science's good fortune that a Paris drama critic realized Bernard's talents lay elsewhere. He recognized the young man's great potential and encouraged him to go to medical school rather than pursue a literary career. Bernard eventually became a professor of physiology at the Sorbonne, then had his own scientific laboratory at France's famous Museum of Natural History in the Jardin des Plantes.

Bernard, working in France at the same time as Pasteur, developed the idea of internal regulation. He thought of blood as an internal environment in which the cells functioned. Bernard first believed that the constancy of this environment was independent of external factors and that maintaining it at a constant level was a major responsibility of all body functions.

## Milieu intérieur

Early in his research, Bernard thought it was possible for the body to regulate itself without the influence of temperature, food, water, or other outside forces. At first, he thought that the plasma of the blood was the total internal environment. Then he expanded his notion to include the lymphatic fluids. He finally came to believe that all the circulating fluids of the organism made up the internal environment, which he called the *milieu intérieur.*[2]

Bernard showed that humans are "a piece of constancy moving in a world of variables."[3] If the interior environment lost its ability to maintain constancy or equilibrium, then the body would lose its ability to function.[4] The body has complex regulatory mechanisms, and its composition must be controlled within very fine limits.[5]

To maintain the constancy of the internal environment, Bernard said, our bodies must do the following:
- Always have the right amount of nutrients and fluids.
- Convert that which it cannot use to a useful product.
- Eliminate that which cannot be converted.
- Eliminate what is in excess.[6]

Bernard's concept of the *milieu intérieur* grew as he learned about the liver's function in cleansing the body. He also realized the importance of the endocrine glands in regulating the interior environment. He found that one role of these glands is to transform ingested food into nutrients and store them for future secretion into the bloodstream. The main purpose of these secretions is to ensure that the blood supply has the consistent chemical atmosphere that is necessary for health.[7]

His research showed that glucose was present in the blood whether it was supplied by the diet or not. This convinced him that the composition of the blood is not solely dependent upon whatever substances we obtain from food. It is the secretions of the liver and glands, not the diet, that give constant properties to the blood.[8]

Bernard also found that temperature played a large role in muscle function. By placing a thermometer into several major arteries and veins, he found that the average temperature remained constant. If the temperature of the blood went above or below a well-defined range, the body would stop functioning. Within this range, the function declined as it approached either the high or low limits.[9] Bernard's ideas on this balance in the body can be summarized as: "All of the vital mechanisms, however varied they may be, have always but one goal, to maintain the uniformity of the conditions of life in the internal environment."[10]

Bernard found that repeating the temperature experiments with different animals yielded different results. These results depended upon the digestive state, general physical condition, and other factors in comparable animals. He felt that all these conditions needed to be addressed when doing experiments on animals.[11]

> This is why it is hard to control research projects. Although it is possible to control the food a participant eats during a research project, it is difficult to control his or her emotions, physical well-being, or other factors. Therefore, much research into nutrition can be deceiving and possibly false.

Finally, after years of experiments and discussions on the

subject, Bernard realized that external conditions, such as diet and other factors, constantly alter the properties of the blood and the *milieu intérieur* in general. Also, internal mechanisms counteract these influences by acting in the opposite direction. The body has the ability to adapt to external conditions, to counter-balance these exterior influences. For example, when the temperature changes, animals are able to change the rate of their own heat production through their skin.[12] When there is less food, the body can preserve what it has. This is the beginning of the feedback system of body chemistry described in Chapter 2. Bernard came to realize that there was a rapid interaction between the individual and the environment. There were also counterbalancing responses of the organisms. Bernard did not believe, as Pasteur did, that life and disease were distinct oppositional forces.[13]

More than one hundred years ago, Bernard understood how important vitamins and minerals were to the functions of the blood in particular and to the body in general. He also recognized the importance of removing waste products from the blood. Waste products could build up from toxins from the environment—from the food, air, and water—and had to be eliminated from the body.

The internal environment simultaneously connected the tissues with the exterior and protected them from the external environment. It was both a link and a barrier for the body to function correctly. All the mechanisms that regulate internal conditions must compensate for both external and internal variations.

## Bernard and Pasteur: A World Apart

Although Claude Bernard and Louis Pasteur lived and worked in France in the same scientific community, they reached very different conclusions about the fundamental nature of disease. One of these differences was whether the pathogen or the host was essential in the beginning of infectious disease. When he died in 1878, Bernard left unpublished note-books that were later published in a scientific journal. This research showed that fermentation does not originate from exterior germs, but that the alcohol is formed by a soluble, life-less ferment in ripe or rotting fruits.[14] This idea is in direct contradiction to Pasteur's theory, which stated that germs from the air caused the ferments.

Unlike Pasteur, who believed that germs lived in the air, Bernard felt that no organic elements could live directly in the air. He believed they would perish without water, or fall dor-mant into a "latent" state.[15] (This state of latency is discussed further in Chapter 5.)

Bernard was so highly regarded for his lifetime contribu-tions to science and medicine that, after his death in 1878, the French government paid tribute to him with a public funeral. It was an unprecedented honor never before bestowed on a person of science, and one denied to Louis Pasteur.[16]

While writing her award-winning doctoral dissertation in 1984, French pharmacist, Marie Nonclercq, came across an unidentified book on the history of medicine. In this book she read that, on his deathbed, Louis Pasteur declared, "Claude Bernard was right . . . the microbe is nothing, the terrain is everything."[17] Whether or not Pasteur actually spoke these words, they accurately sum up Bernard's discoveries.

At the same time that Pasteur was forming the germ theory, there were others, among them Claude Bernard, who did not view disease as caused by an outside invader. These researchers believed it was the condition of the organism that placed the organism in jeopardy of disease. Another French scientist, Antoine Béchamp, developed this idea further, as we will see in the next chapter.

## A Woman's View of Disease

Pioneering English nurse Florence Nightingale (1820-1910) is renowned throughout the world for her work as a reformer of hospital conditions, a humanitarian, and a writer. She also shared Claude Bernard's view that disease was a condition rather than an entity unto itself.

Without scientific research, but with a great deal of hands-on research in the squalid conditions of war, she made observations that are very similar to those of Bernard. She summarized the origins of disease in her famous book, *Notes on Nursing.*

"Is it not living in a continual mistake, to look upon diseases, as we do now, as separate entities, which must exist, like cats and dogs, instead of looking upon them as conditions like a dirty or clean condition, and just as much under our own control; or rather as the reactions . . . against the conditions in which we have placed ourselves? I was brought up by scientific men and ignorant women distinctly to believe that smallpox was a thing of which there was once a specimen in the world, which went on propagating itself in a perpetual chain of descent, just as much as that there was a first dog (or a first pair of dogs) and that smallpox would not begin itself any more than a new dog would begin without there having been a parent dog. Since then I have seen with my eyes and smelt with my nose smallpox growing up in first specimens, either in close rooms or in overcrowded wards, where it would not by any possibility have been 'caught' but must have begun. Nay, more, I have seen diseases begin, grow up and pass into one another. New dogs do not pass into cats. I have seen, for instance, with a little overcrowding, continued fever grow up, and with a little more, typhoid fever, and with a little more, typhus, and all in the same ward or hut. For diseases, as all experience shows, are adjectives, not noun substantives. . . The specific disease doctrine is the grand refuge of weak, uncultured, unstable minds, such as now rule in the medical profession. There are no specific diseases; there are specific disease conditions."[18]

CHAPTER 5

# ANTOINE BÉCHAMP AND THE PLEOMORPHIC THEORY OF DISEASE

*Disease is born of us and in us.*
Antoine Béchamp (1816-1908)[1]

Working in the same scientific community as Louis Pasteur and Claude Bernard was Antoine Béchamp, a medical doctor, doctor of science in chemistry, master of pharmacy, and a university professor of physics, toxicology, medical chemistry, and biochemistry. He was the author of several medical books about the blood and disease, and his articles were widely published.

Béchamp and Pasteur were conducting much of the same research simultaneously. Like Pasteur and Bernard, Béchamp spoke at conferences and reported his research to the Academy of Sciences, the Academy of Medicine, and other distinguished groups. But underlying this camaraderie was a continual controversy between the basic concepts of Pasteur and Béchamp.

# Béchamp's Little Bodies

While Béchamp occasionally acted as an assistant to Pasteur, his own research into fermentation led him to a different theory about the cause of disease.[2] In one of his early fermentation experiments, Béchamp used commercial chalk, to which he had added sugar and creosote to suppress the influence of atmospheric germs. The commercial chalk, which was made in the laboratory under artificial conditions, did not ferment. Béchamp then repeated the experiment using chemically pure calcium carbonate with sugar and creosote. This time, the chalk fermented[3] He realized there was something in the natural chalk that was not present in the artificial chalk. He called these organized and living ferments "little bodies," or microzymas. They acted like molds and were agents of fermentation.[4]

Béchamp continued other experiments with different media. His research showed that throughout the cells of living organisms there are much smaller units—and there are millions of them. These microzymas are present in the cells in the bloodstream, in plants, in every living thing.[5] They organize and nourish all the cells of life forms at the molecular level. They are elementary units in all living structures, as well as the controlling factor in the cells of all animal and plant life.[6]

Although usually healthy, microzymas can develop into the disease-producing bacteria, viruses, and fungus that can lead to chronic and degenerative illness. Béchamp believed these little bodies were pleomorphic, changing form continually when they were both healthy and diseased.[7] According to the scientific theory of pleomorphism, bacteria change and take on multiple forms during a single life cycle. In much the same way as a caterpillar grows into a butterfly or a tadpole develops into a frog, the microzymas can change both form and function.

Béchamp did not believe in Pasteur's idea about monomorphism, that microorganisms do not change form. Béchamp's microzymas differed from Pasteur's microorganisms in that

Pasteur's species were fixed and eternal. Each microorganism was associated with a specific disease, and there were a finite number of them.[8]

Béchamp also questioned the notion that germs were specially created organisms, appearing mysteriously in the atmosphere. He felt they were evolutionary forms of microzymas that built up in the cells of plants and animals. Microzymas may evolve into bacteria, and bacteria may again be reduced to microzymas. In the human body, healthy microzymas could become unhealthy, then go back to being healthy again.

## The Cat in the Jar

One of Béchamp's pivotal experiments was carried out in 1868, in Montpellier in southern France, far from Paris and Pasteur. Béchamp completely covered the dead body of a cat in pure calcium carbonate and creosote. He then placed the cat in a glass jar with sheets of paper over the mouth of the jar. This allowed the air to circulate but kept out dust and germs. Eight years later, nothing remained of the body but some dried matter and a few fragments of bone. The cat's remains gave off no odor.

Looking through the microscope, Béchamp could see the shining microzymas. He noted that they were only found in the layers near the spot where he had laid the cat's body. However, they were there in abundance. "They swarmed in their thousands in every field of the microscope," he observed.[9]

To refute any possible objections, Béchamp used more precautions when he repeated the experiment in June of 1875, in Lille, in northern France. He replaced the creosote with phenolic acid to suppress the influence of atmospheric germs. He also expanded the scope of the experiment, using the whole cadaver of a small cat, the liver of another cat, and the lungs, hearts, and kidneys of several other cats.

Seven years later, in August of 1882, he observed that the

same fermentation was taking place in all the experiments, but to a lesser degree. He attributed this slower fermentation to Lille's cooler temperatures. He concluded that the microzymas in the tissues of the cadavers had evolved and produced bacteria.[10] The bacteria could not have come from the atmosphere, as Pasteur's theory stated.

## The Cell Is Not Ultimate

While many scientists at the time followed the dictum of German pathologist Rudolf Virchow, "Only from cells arise cells," Béchamp found that the cell is not ultimate. Instead, it is made up of even more primitive units. Under certain conditions, the germ may be a product, a result, an effect of the disease process. The body becomes toxic; then healthy bacteria in the body become unhealthy. This metamorphosis need not be the result of an outside invader, as Pasteur suggested. **Under certain unhealthy conditions, the infection is exclusively an endogenous process. It comes from within the body itself.**

Disease can manifest itself in another way. Germs that come from within can be given to someone else. Germs can live in the air for a short time. If someone who is sick sneezes on you and has a germ, that germ can spread to you. If you do get sick from another person's germs, the illness should be short-lived, a simple illness. If a cold or flu lingers with a cough, runny nose, sneezes and other symptoms for days, you know that you have a weakened immune system. The immune system has a lowered resistance, is not strong, and is probably dealing with other problems as well as the cold. (We will discuss this further when we look at the work of Dr. Melvin Page in Chapter 7.)

When the body is out of homeostasis, its resistance to disease is lowered. This lowered resistance can allow a germ to enter. Under other conditions, a lowered resistance in the body occurs before an antigen (an exogenous factor, from outside the body) is added into the mix. This second "injury" becomes double trouble.[11] As Béchamp wrote, "What eats us and destroys us after death is that same thing that lived in us, without us . . . Life is a succession of little deaths, or, if you prefer, a continued putrefaction."[12]

Pasteur believed that bacteria die when they are deprived of oxygen. Béchamp believed the microzymas did not die in the absence of oxygen; they simply went into a state of rest, a dormant state. He found microzymas in fetuses and in all organs of the body. Later, he showed that the little bodies had various forms and actions in different organs. His research demonstrated that no outside creature or bacteria was necessary to cause these changes. No outside germ was necessary for a healthy person to become sick. The microzymas could also undergo bacterial evolution in the body without becoming diseased. They persisted both before and after the death of their host.[13] When an organism dies, its cells disappear, but the microzymas remain imperishable.[14]

Unhealthy bacteria can develop from microzymas by passing through certain intermediate stages. In these intermediate stages, bacteria can become other species of bacteria, fungus, or other destructive forms in the body.[15] Béchamp thought these changes from healthy to unhealthy forms depended upon the toxicity of the terrain—the toxicity of the body. Pasteur, on the other hand, believed that the body had a physiochemical composition and nothing else. He felt there was nothing inherently alive in the composition of animals and vegetables. His intent was to show that meat, milk, blood, and wine would remain unchanged if they were not exposed to any air at all.[16] This idea was in direct opposition to what Béchamp believed.

One of Béchamp's experiments showed that meat would become tainted even if it was not exposed to air and was kept under perfectly sterile conditions. When Pasteur repeated the same experiment, he used every precaution possible to prevent contamination by germ-containing air. Even so, the muscle of the meat became tainted. Pasteur dismissed the experiment with a vague explanation, saying it was "power of transformation."[17]

> It is hard to believe that a hard-core scientist would say something like this. I do not think that anyone knew what it meant.

Béchamp believed that fermentation was the process of nutrition, assimilation, metabolism, and excretion of a product that was a natural part of the body.[18] It was part of the life and death process. Pasteur believed fermentation was correlated with the development and organization of germs from the outside, not with their death and decomposition.

The germs of disease cannot exist primarily in clean air, healthy food, or in water that is pure. Every disease proceeds from a sick environment. Diseased microzymas may be found in unhealthy air, earth, or water, in unhealthy humans, animals, and plants, and in the remains of humans, animals, and plants.

> The plant world is a good illustration of this: a healthy plant does not have insects, but an unhealthy plant attracts insects.

Béchamp extracted microzymas from rocks that were thousands of years old, proving that these tiny bodies could live in a dormant state for practically unlimited periods of time. The microzymas he found in rocks were the same as those he found in human cells.[19] He believed that minute living entities were present in all forms of life, from the smallest one-celled amoebae to humans. These microzymas were necessary for cells to grow and repair themselves. Two American scientists confirmed his findings in 1974 when they discovered bacteria in soil and rock samples taken from depths varying between 290 and 1,400 feet. Geologists dated the samples from 10,000 to 1,000,000 years. After the bacteria thawed out, all but one strain revived, grew, and reproduced.[20]

Béchamp believed that when the medium, terrain, or body chemistry in a human became toxic to normal microzymas, these microzymas would change healthy bacteria into unhealthy bacteria or germs. Unlike Pasteur, who thought that bacteria were the origins of the disease process, Béchamp felt that bacteria were the unhealthy consequence, not the origin, of the disease condition. He realized that, in the evolution of disease, the terrain (the interior environment, the body chemistry) was far more important than the germ.[21]

> What causes the terrain to become unsuitable for normal microzymas? What triggers healthy microzymas to change into diseased forms? Instead of being at the mercy of outside enemies, the microzymas change forms all by themselves, in a toxic interior. Microzymas can become diseased entities as a result of what we eat, think, say, do, and feel. They can also become toxic because of chemicals in the air, water, soil, food, and many other factors of our lifestyle. When we upset our body chemistry through the indiscretions of our twentieth century lifestyle, it reflects on the microzymas. Their corruption afterwards avenges itself upon us. When too many microzymas become diseased, the immune system becomes overwhelmed and can no longer function optimally. The body then becomes prey to so-called opportunistic diseases.

On the last page of *The Blood and Its Third Anatomical Element*, Béchamp wrote emphatically about what he had been observing for years.

After death, it is essential that matter is restored to its primitive condition, for it has only been lent for a time to the living organized being. . . . The living being, filled with microzymas, carries in himself the elements essential for life, for disease, for death and for destruction. This variety in results may not too much surprise us, the processes are the same. Our [cells], it is a matter of constant observation, are being continually destroyed by means of a fermentation very analogous to that which follows death. Penetrating into the heart of these phenomena we might say, were it not for the offensiveness of the expression, that we are constantly rotting.[22]

In the years following his discoveries, Béchamp had strong support in the scientific community for his observations about pleomorphism. Researcher Dr. Ernst Bernhard Almquist (1852-1946) documented hundreds of observations of pleomorphic bacteria in his laboratory. "Nobody can pretend to know the complete life cycle and all the varieties of even a single bacterial species," Dr. Almquist concluded. "It would be an assumption to think so."[23] Along with researchers in Italy, Russia, France, Germany, and the United States, Almquist saw what Pasteur could not seem to see.

> Disease is toxicity, and a toxic body can become diseased. We can stop much of the "rotting" by ceasing to upset our body chemistry. When our body chemistry is in homeostasis, we create health, not disease.

## Pasteur and Béchamp: A Study in Contrasts

Béchamp and Pasteur disagreed strongly about what caused disease, as is evident in their papers, correspondence, and addresses to scientific meetings.

What Pasteur believed about disease:

- Germs are found everywhere in the air, and these atmospheric organisms are the cause of fermentation, putrefaction, and human diseases.[24]

- Normal healthy animals have bacteriologically sterile tissues. Bacteria are not normally found within the body proper. Contamination, the invasion of external germs, causes putrefaction.[25]

- Bacteria are monomorphic and do not change form. For example, cocci (spherical shaped bacteria) could not become rods.[26]

- Fermentation, decomposition, and putrefaction are physicochemical rather than vital processes.[27]

- Cells are the elementary units of life.[28]

- Spontaneous generation does not occur.[29]

- Each type of bacterium is a distinct species, and these species alone cause a corresponding specific disease.[30]

What Béchamp believed about disease:

- Microzymas (tiny molecular granules or small ferments) in the cells of all living matter could develop into disease-producing bacteria and lead to chronic illness.[31]

- All living things are filled with microzymas and, therefore, are bacterial in nature.

- Microzymas are pleomorphic. They can change and take on multiple forms during a single life cycle by changing the conditions of the environment.[32]

- The ferments in the juice of the grape are organic in origin, and these same ferments cause all animal and vegetable matter to putrefy. Putrefaction is due to a change in the microzymas.[33] Fermentation, decomposition, and putrefaction are vital forces.[34]

- Microzymas are the elementary units of life and the builders of cell tissues.[35]

- Spontaneous generation does occur but not from nothing; rather, it occurs as a result of a change in the microzymas that are always with us.[36]

Pasteur's ideas eventually won out for many reasons, principally because he was such a tireless self-promoter. At every step of the way, he made himself known to his peers in the scientific community and to the public. Béchamp never sought the attention Pasteur received. He was first and foremost a scientist who spent much of his time in his laboratory. He was not interested in adulation.

Pasteur's concept about germs was disarmingly simple. Each disease was connected to a certain germ. This makes for a simple-looking solution to a complex problem: Just find the right antidote for each germ and disease will vanish. Béchamp's concept was more difficult. Because bacteria change form, it is more difficult to diagnose disease.

This was an era when scientists thought that nature could be conquered. It has certainly been proven often enough that we can't conquer nature. Far from it! One hundred years after the introduction of Pasteur's germ theory—the discovery that was going to wipe out illness—infectious and degenerative diseases still escape our grasp and are increasing.

Perhaps it isn't necessary to know the varieties of bacterial species. Today, many bacteriologists admit there are no fixed species. Even in strictly controlled laboratory environments, maintaining fixed, typical cultures is difficult; the bacteria will change both form and function quite readily.[37] It would be more important, and more useful, to find out what an individual is doing wrong that is causing bacterial species that normally have a healthy growth in the body to become unhealthy and cause disease.

## Conclusions

Béchamp was ahead of his time in the conclusions he reached about the cause of disease. He was also well respected for his ideas; his list of medical journal articles and correspondence with scientific academies covers ten pages.[38] Unfortunately, when Pasteur's germ theory became the ruling medical paradigm, Béchamp's considerable body of research was put aside and forgotten.

The neglect he has suffered from medical historians has outraged those who have championed his ideas. As the authors of *Rational Bacteriology* wrote, "To delete from history's pages the record of Béchamp's work is on a par with the crime of those physicians who prepared the hemlock cup for Socrates."[39] This sentiment was echoed by the German scientist Guenther Enderlein (see Chapter 8), author of a classic work on the life cycle of bacteria. As far as Enderlein was concerned, "biological research was diverted down the wrong road."[40] Writing in 1990, the historical medical writer Alan Cantwell summed up his own research on Pasteur and Béchamp as follows:

> My study of Béchamp had shattered the icon of Pasteur. The chemist made germs respectable and he was a genius at popularizing microbes as a cause of human disease. . . . he also put science on the wrong track. Pasteur's dogma transformed the art and science of medicine into a multibillion dollar bio-technical business in search of the perfect pill and the perfect vaccine to cure man of all his ills. . . . In the process the physicians were blinded.[41]

Béchamp's research paved the way for other scientists who viewed disease pleomorphically. The spirit of his work was also carried on by those researchers who believed, as he did, that an unhealthy immune system, not invasive germs, was the cause of disease. In the next chapter we will look at the work of American physiologist Walter B. Cannon, who coined the term "homeostasis" and increased our understanding of the role that the endocrine and digestive systems play in maintaining good health. We'll also see how Cannon extended Claude Bernard's idea of the *milieu intérieur*.

CHAPTER 6

# WALTER B. CANNON'S THEORY OF HOMEOSTASIS

*Only by understanding the wisdom of the body . . .*
*shall we attain the mastery of disease and pain that*
*will enable us to relieve the burden of people.*
Walter Bradford Cannon (1871-1945)[1]

It seems appropriate that Walter Bradford Cannon would be the scientist who contributed so much to our understanding of the body's system for maintaining balance. He was a man whose life was defined by balance. A brilliant physiologist, he was equally at home working in his research laboratory and hiking in the mountains. (Glacier National Park's Mount Cannon is named in his honor.) He was a serious academic whose best research ideas came to him while he was watching Harvard football games. As well as serving in World War One, Cannon gave much of his time and energy to providing medical aid to war-torn countries and relief to suffering refugees. Throughout his life, he maintained a deep concern for the rights and liberties of others.

Although Cannon coined the term "homeostasis" in the mid-1920s, he did not explain it fully until 1932, when he wrote his extraordinary book, *The Wisdom of the Body*. He defined homeostasis as the coordinated physiological process that maintains most of the steady states in the body. The process is directed by the endocrine system, which secretes hormones into the bloodstream to help regulate this steady state, keeping it in dynamic equilibrium.

Cannon solidified his concept of homeostasis by learning from other researchers. His work incorporated the findings of Claude Bernard, psychologists William James and Carl Lange, physiologist J.S. Haldane, and Sir Frederick G. Banting and Charles H. Best, the discoverers of insulin. Even so, much of Cannon's research has not received its due. Like the discoveries of Claude Bernard and Antoine Béchamp, Cannon's work has been overlooked because of modern medicine's emphasis on disease and cures rather than on the functioning and malfunctioning of the body.

## A Pioneer in the Study of Digestion

Few people today realize what Cannon knew a hundred years ago about the importance of digestion to health. Cannon first became interested in the physiology and mechanics of digestion while he was an undergraduate at Harvard, and his fascination with the subject grew when he was in medical school.[2]

He was encouraged in his studies by Henry Bickering Bowditch, chairman of Harvard's physiology department in the 1880s and 1890s, who became his scientific father and guiding light. Bowditch also introduced his young student to the work of Claude Bernard, with whom he had studied in France. Bernard's concept of the *milieu intérieur* intrigued Cannon and was a significant influence in his later work. Cannon wrote about Bernard in *The Wisdom of the Body*. Throughout his long career at Harvard, he kept on his wall a framed print of the forgotten French scientist instructing a group of students.

Under Bowditch's guidance, Cannon made the first of his many discoveries about digestion. He found that carbohydrates leave the stomach far more rapidly than a protein meal and that fat remains in the stomach longer than any other type of food.[3]

With Wilhelm Roentgen's discovery of the X-ray in 1895, Cannon was able to expand his studies of the digestive tract.[4] After much research, he learned how to obtain satisfactory X-ray pictures of the soft organs of the digestive tract. He would mix his patients' food with bismuth subnitrate or barium sulfate, both of which are opaque to X-rays. Every modern hospital in the world was soon using this technique to diagnose gastric ulcers and tumors of the digestive tract.

Cannon was the first to observe and write about peristalsis, the contraction of the muscles of the stomach and small intestines that moves the food through the digestive tract. He noted that the shape of the stomach changed dramatically during digestion. He also discovered that when a cat becomes afraid or enraged, the peristaltic movements in the stomach halt briefly and digestion stops. When the movements stop, the stomach can change shape even more. It may swell up and become distended because the food is not moving through. In fact, all the digestive activities in the gut become extremely sensitive to nervous conditions such as anger or fear.[5]

## Learning from a Football Game

Speculating that the human digestive system also responded to nervous conditions, Cannon took his research to the football field. Before a Harvard/Yale football game, he X-rayed the stomachs of the Harvard players and a control group of non-players, making sure there was no food in their digestive tracts. Both groups then ate the usual pre-game meal served to the football players. The control group went home, and the football players went ahead with their game. About two and a half hours later, when the game was over, Cannon X-rayed both groups again. The players still had most of the food in their digestive tracts, but the meal had already gone through the digestive tracts of the control group. The experiment showed how intense emotions can stop the peristaltic action and digestion.

All of this research culminated in Cannon's 1911 book *The Mechanical Factors of Digestion*, which focused on nutrition and the effects of the emotions on nutrition.[6]

> At the beginning of the century, Cannon understood how emotions could affect digestion. He was one of the first to look at what we now know as psychoneuroimmunology, which studies the effects that psychological factors, the nerves, and body chemistry have on the immune system. This is another important concept that was neglected because of the focus on the germ theory. Few doctors, medical students, or the public took notice.

## Cannon's Investigation into Emotions

Cannon moved from the study of emotions and digestion to the study of the physiology of emotions in general. He was intrigued by Charles Darwin's book *Expressions of the Emotions in Man and Animals*, which documented animals showing anger, fear and other emotions. The English naturalist did not explain what impact these negative emotions had on the animals' bodies; nor was he concerned with what caused these emotions.[7] Cannon was most interested in the cause of emotions and in the effects these negative emotions had on the internal environment. He was greatly influenced by the work of psychologists William James and Carl Lange, who showed that emotions were directly connected to the involuntary psychological changes triggered by exciting situations.[8]

Next, Cannon corresponded with and met Ivan Pavlov, the Russian scientist who was renowned for his studies on dogs. Pavlov showed that dogs respond to stress in highly individualized ways. Put in an identical stressful situation, they will react according to their own nature and their particular experience. Cannon understood that this finding had important implications for human behavior as well. If an individual viewed an experience as negative, it could cause psychological stress and result in severe and long-lasting functional disorders.[9]

Although you may not be in control of situations that present themselves, you are responsible for how you react to those situations. You can see how situations can have either little effect or an overwhelming effect on your body, depending on how you view them. We can all watch the same building burn to the ground and come away with different observations and emotions. Depending on how we deal with it psychologically, the fire could have lingering consequences, or we could quickly put the experience behind us. A highly-charged emotional experience may lead to a severe disorder, or it may have no lasting impact at all.

Cannon began to realize that many activities of the organs were under the control of sympathetic nerves. We have little control over these involuntary nerves that act upon the organs of the body. Still, Cannon found that animals continue to have physiological consequences, symptoms such as high blood pressure, digestive or neurological problems, long after an emotional disturbance has occurred.

Cannon then realized that the hormone adrenaline was responsible for prolonging these disturbances even after the immediate stimulus had disappeared. Following this line of reasoning, he became the first to show the relationship between the secretion of hormones into the bloodstream and the physiology of emotions.[10]

## The Fight or Flight Syndrome

In 1914, Cannon established that adrenaline helped to divert blood from the organs of the abdomen to the heart, lungs, central nervous system, and limbs. The process of digestion could wait until the immediate crisis was over, and until the extra energy it required was needed elsewhere in the body. He also found that adrenaline helped to remedy muscular fatigue, hastened the coagulation of blood when the body is wounded, and cooperated with sympathetic nerves in bringing sugar stored in the liver back into the bloodstream to supply extra energy.

Some of his experiments showed that the adrenaline secreted into the bloodstream in a dangerous situation elicited responses from the cardiovascular, respiratory, muscular, metabolic, and hematological systems. All of the phenomena of the "fight/flight syndrome"—the body's automatic response to danger or an emergency—add to our ability to survive in perilous situations.

From his reading of *Introduction to Social Psychology*, by the psychologist William Douglass, Cannon understood that fear correlated with the instinct to flee and anger with an instinct to fight.[11] Ever since Cannon explained these ideas, his "emergency" theory of the physiology of emotions has dominated all discussions of the fight/flight syndrome.[12] With the publication of his 1915 book, *Bodily Changes in Pain, Hunger, Fear and Rage*, he became the first to show the relationship between the secretion of hormones into the bloodstream and the physiology of emotions.[13]

> Adrenaline is extremely important, but many of us have exhausted our adrenal glands. We have too much sugar, caffeine and other unhealthy food in our diet, and we allow our stress to become distress. All of this leads to an imbalance in the endocrine system. When one gland becomes depleted, other glands have to compensate by secreting more of their hormone. The whole delicate hormonal balance becomes upset. This problem can be alleviated if we deal with the stress, stop eating junk food, exercise regularly, and remove as many toxic chemicals as we can from our bodies and our environment.

# The Influence of Strong Emotions on the Body

Cannon's understanding of the fight/flight syndrome and the physiological response to stress was enriched by his own experiences in World War One.[14]   When he went to war in 1917, he encountered many cases of "soldier's heart." Under the intolerable stresses of war, he concluded, the sympathetic control of the heart often became over-sensitized to even the mildest stimulation. This resulted in paralysis rather than energy.

Cannon saw the toll that war took on the body and on the emotions. At the same time, he felt the sedentary twentieth-century lifestyle provided no adequate release for the human adrenaline rush or for the fight/flight syndrome.

> Imagine what Cannon would think of our lifestyle today!

He was very convinced by William James's description of "reservoirs of power, not under normal conditions drawn upon but ready to pour forth streams of energy in a crisis."[15]   Cannon did not want to repress these emotions; instead, he felt that people needed a healthy way to use them.

Again, he found the answer to his question at a Harvard/Yale football game. Cannon observed that, at any intense game, the spectators experienced a surge of power and energy along with the athletes. The spectators, too, would feel exhilarated and self-confident. At these highly charged, emotional times, Cannon found, the spectators and the players all had sugar in their urine. The rush of adrenaline brought additional sugar from the liver into the bloodstream and the excess into the urine.[16]

Researchers have since found that caffeine also triggers adrenaline to mobilize stored sugar from the liver into the bloodstream. Taking caffeine has the same effect as adrenaline does. Both a rush of adrenaline and the ingestion of caffeine bring sugar to the bloodstream to give you "a lift." This added sugar in the bloodstream and excessive stress to the body can exhaust the adrenal glands.

Like the psychologist William Douglass, Cannon believed that humans had aggressive instincts that they used in time of need. Unfortunately, these aggressive instincts were too often used destructively. "How do you show people how to use these emotions constructively?" Cannon wondered.

In 1929, he put out a new edition of *Bodily Changes in Pain, Hunger, Fear and Rage*.[17] This time, he played down the idea that strong emotions could be an advantage. He realized that excessive emotions could often cause damaging or even fatal results, literally consuming the person who expressed them. These excesses could manifest themselves in physical disease—a heart attack or degenerative disease—as well as in psychological illness.

Cannon observed that fear, worry, rage and resentment left no obvious structural changes in the brain or nerves. But if these negative emotions continued, an individual's facial expressions and body language could be lastingly affected, and so could their internal organs, in particular the stomach and the intestines. Cannon called such lasting effects "habitual emotional expressions." These expressions could become fixed and alter the functioning of the organs, causing illness and even becoming life-threatening. As researchers since Cannon have found, negative emotions have real power to upset the body's healthy processes and homeostasis. Since that time, researchers have found that these emotions can also have grave negative effects on the bloodstream and the immune system.

If you are constantly stressed in your job, you may not realize that any symptoms you might be having, such as headaches, joint pains, stomach aches, acid stomach etc., are caused by the stress. Continuous psychological distress can slowly increase symptoms and lead to degenerative disease.[18] Even in Cannon's time, the mind-body connection seemed so clear, but few recognized it.

Cannon had come to understand that emotionally troubled patients could help themselves only by discovering why they were haunted by their anxieties and conflicts. Negative emotions could cause physical symptoms and chronic and degenerative diseases, and the patients had to see the correlation between their distress and their symptoms. In spite of his alternative view of sickness, Cannon remained a loyal member of the orthodox medical community. He believed it was important to explore every other possible explanation for illness before turning to emotional factors.

Cannon's insights could have moved him in a new direction, but he was a physiologist by education, by profession, and—most importantly—by temperament. He therefore continued his study of physiology rather than integrating the disciplines of physiology and abnormal psychology.

## Beginnings of the Concept of Homeostasis

Cannon's studies had taken him from digestion to the adrenal gland and adrenaline, then to the sympathetic system and, finally, to the autonomic system in general. All his research had made him aware of the self-regulatory processes of the body. He now understood that the body was continually adapting to environmental challenges, giving signals or showing symptoms to try to remedy any deviation from its stable state. These signals included sneezes, wheezes, congestion, headaches, stomach aches, joint pains, fatigue and skin problems—to name a few. He realized that for every action that took the body away from the stable state, there was an opposite reaction to bring it back.

Cannon felt that higher animals could achieve and maintain stability under all but the most serious external conditions. He coined the term "homeostasis" to refer to the coordinated physiological process that maintains most of the steady states in the body, and he recognized that the process is directed by the endocrine system.

> The endocrine system is made up of glands that release hormones into the bloodstream. The pituitary gland serves to regulate and maintain the secretion of hormones. Other important glands are the adrenals, thyroid, gonads (ovaries and testes), and pancreas. Today, many of us have endocrine problems. We upset our body chemistry through our twentieth century lifestyle, by eating unhealthy foods, letting stress become distress, and not exercising. This taxes our endocrine system, and the glands may secrete too much of some hormones and not enough of others. The consequences of underactive glands include the need for insulin for diabetics and thyroxin for an underactive thyroid gland. Some people have exhausted their adrenals, which causes exhaustion, dizziness, excess perspiration, and lightheadedness.
>
> There are so many factors in our lifestyle that upset our body chemistry that some of us have difficulty regaining and maintaining homeostasis. Our bodies only have so many reserves. Our reserves are our body's organs and glands that have the ability to deal with crisis situations. Because of today's stressful lifestyle, our bodies have to respond to many—too many—of these crisis situations. When we are continually upsetting our body chemistry, we deplete those reserves. The homeostatic mechanisms are overloaded and cannot operate optimally. This is when the symptoms become a presence in our lives. Chronic fatigue sets in. Allergies become a problem. Our joints hurt. We have frequent headaches. Yeast infections need to be treated. These symptoms can then lead to more serious problems, such as heart disease, diabetes, cancer, and arthritis. Psychological and physical stress can also upset the internal environment and make it toxic.

# The Feedback System

With his understanding of homeostasis, Cannon went on to study the feedback system, which was described by French physiologist Charles Richet as follows:

> The living being is stable. It must be in order not to be destroyed, dissolved or disintegrated by the colossal forces, often adverse, which surround it. By an apparent contradiction, it maintains its stability only if it is excitable and capable of modifying itself according to external stimuli and adjusting its response to the stimulation. In a sense it is stable because it is modifiable. The slight instability is the necessary condition for the true stability of the organism.[19]

Because the whole process of homeostasis is a feedback system, when it is off-kilter, it can feed back substances that make a person sick. Whatever disease develops depends on which tissue malfunctions or becomes toxic.

Table I on the next page is an example of the feedback mechanism in the body and how one event "feeds back" a series of responses.

When the body is unable to maintain a healthy homeostasis, the feedback system, which is regulated by the endocrine system, cannot function optimally. The glands do not secrete the correct amount of hormones, and the body chemistry becomes upset. The body's ability to fend off foreign invaders and environmental toxins becomes impaired, and the vicious cycle begins.

# Defining Homeostasis and its Principles

Cannon was not the only researcher who saw the importance of balance in the body. Many others were carrying out research that pointed in the same basic direction. His gift lay in his ability to synthesize and advance ideas, to blend his work with the work of others into a cohesive whole. He replaced Claude Bernard's unwieldy notion of the milieu intérieur with the concept of a "fluid matrix" that was affected by both the external and internal environments. Cannon also discovered that the levels of sugar and calcium in the blood had to remain within a very narrow range or there would be major consequences throughout the body. (We'll talk about this more in the next chapter on Melvin Page.)

## Feedback Mechanisms and Endocrine Control of Homeostasis

| | | |
|---|---|---|
| Clean | External Environment | Poisonous |
| Healthy | Internal Environment | Toxic |
| Function Optimally | Homeostatic Mechanisms | Become Less Functioning |
| Work Optimally | Endocrine Glands | Unable to Work Properly |
| Correct Amount of Hormones | Secrete Hormones | Too Little or Too Much of a Hormone |
| Hormones Are Received by Target Organs | Target Organs | Hormones Are Less Able to Be Received by Target Organs |
| Maintain Homeostasis | Homeostasis | Lose Ability to Maintain Homeostasis |

**Cannon's Definition of Homeostasis:**

Homeostasis designates the stability of the body.

Homeostatic conditions indicate details of the stability.

Homeostatic reactions signify the means for maintaining stability.

# Cannon's Six Principles of Homeostasis:

Cannon identified these six principles of homeostasis. He did not believe they were exhaustive. He considered them to be tentative and hoped they would lead to further investigation into human physiology.

1. The body is an open system, which means it is affected by the outside environment. Our bodies have automatic biochemical systems that are open and can be enhanced and/or challenged by outside factors such as temperature extremes, food and drink excesses, emotional excesses, and others. Constancy (or homeostasis) is evident because there are systems and organs that act or are ready to act to meet the challenge of an outside stimulus and maintain this constancy. These homeostatic mechanisms include the endocrine system's hormonal agents, the liver, the kidneys, the heart, and other organs which meet the challenge of an outside stimulus. The chemicals used in our food chain are an example of an environmental factor that could affect the body. The liver has the ability to detoxify chemicals and make them into products the body can use.

2. If a homeostatic condition continues, it does so because any tendency toward change is automatically met by an opposing force to help bring the body back to homeostasis. When we eat, some of the food in the digestive system is converted into a simple sugar called glucose. This glucose goes into the bloodstream, raising the glucose level. The pancreas responds by secreting insulin. The insulin enables the body to transfer the

blood glucose into the body's cells. This re-establishes the homeostatic level of blood glucose which helps total body homeostasis.

3. There is no homeostatic agent in the body that has the ability to act in different directions at the same time. Insulin lowers the blood glucose level when the body has more glucose than it needs. Insulin cannot raise the blood sugar level. The pancreas secretes another hormone, glycogen, to raise the blood glucose level when it gets too low. Just as insulin cannot raise the blood sugar level, glycogen cannot lower it.

4. Sometimes homeostatic agents can be antagonistic in one region of the body and cooperative in another. Let's look at insulin again. We need the insulin in the bloodstream after we have eaten carbohydrates to remove the end product of carbohydrates (sugar) and to help get the sugar into the cells. When we are eating too many carbohydrates, the levels of sugar and insulin in the blood are too high. This excess of insulin can cause major problems. It may turn the sugar into fat, promoting excessive body fat gain. High insulin levels also convert calories into triglycerides and cholesterol, which increase the risk of coronary artery disease. When we eat fewer carbohydrates and simple sugars, insulin is a healthy part of the metabolic process. When we eat too many simple sugars, or when other lifestyle factors such as distress interfere with metabolic pathways, the excess insulin can also cause problems in other parts of the body.

5. The body's health is determined by its ability to regulate or balance itself. Sometimes these regulations include a number of cooperating factors that come into action at the same time or successively. Buffer systems regulate the pH (acid/alkalinity) of the blood, which helps to maintain homeostasis. When the pH because too acidic, the body uses mainly the sodium bicarbonate and potassium bicarbonate part of the buffer system to help bring the blood back to a normal pH, or homeostasis. The blood wants to stay in homeostasis continually and will do any-

thing to stay in balance, even at the expense of other parts of the body.

6. If its chemistry is upset due to lifestyle excesses, the body can shift out of the homeostatic state. At that time, it is reasonable to look for another regulating factor in the body to help bring it back to homeostasis. Cannon felt there was always a control in the body so that it would not move far enough out of homeostasis to cause harm. If it moved too far, there was another homeostatic mechanism that would bring it back. This principle repeats the other principles; however, Cannon wanted to emphasize that homeostasis is not accidental—it is a result of the body's ability to regulate itself.

## Cannon and the Germ Theory

If Cannon made a single reference to Pasteur in his data, research, lab notes or correspondence, I was unable to find it. However, his writings show him to be at complete odds with Pasteur's germ theory. He was more aligned with Béchamp's theory of pleomorphism, as is apparent in his statement that "Residing in the mouth and intestines, in the nose, in the skin—indeed, on practically all the surfaces and in practically all the orifices of the body—are myriads of bacteria."[19] For the most part, he said, these bacteria were harmless. But, like Béchamp, he believed they could change and cause inflammation and disease.

Cannon felt there were "cells" in the body that could go dormant rather than die, and he understood the notion of "a general weakened state"—the state that Béchamp believed caused the microzymas to change from healthy to unhealthy. In Cannon's terms, a weakened state might occur when the body is unable to maintain homeostasis. "Perhaps because of failure to keep a part clean, or because of slight injury or some general weakened state," he explained, "pus-producing bacteria, which are living close to the root of a hair in the skin, begin to multiply rapidly."[20]

> How radically opposed to Pasteur's germ invaders is this
> Cannon/Bernard model of the self-regulating machine
> slowly destroying itself in its determination to survive!

## Conclusions

Cannon always had a practical application for his laboratory discoveries, and he was tremendously gifted at communicating his findings to specialists from many disciplines—gastroenterologists, neurologists, surgeons, physicians, psychiatrists, even politicians and social scientists. He would undoubtedly have liked to see a multifaceted approach to the study of disease, a variation of psychoneuroimmunology that encompassed the study of the endocrine and gastrointestinal systems as well. Psycho-neuro-endocrino-gastrointestinal-immunology would have been Cannon's specialty!

As a forerunner in his understanding of psychosomatic medicine, Cannon realized the role that the mind plays in disease. He refuted scientists who look for disease solely in the organs, just as he refuted the germ theorists by showing that disease has more than one cause. His understanding of homeostasis convinced him that the body must be treated as a whole. It will heal itself if put back into homeostasis and given a chance.

In later life, Cannon paid the price for some of his early research. Although the dangers of X-rays were known when he began his studies with the new tool, Cannon did not have this information during the first year of his research. He did not take precautions to protect himself or others from the X-rays.[21] This unwitting oversight came back to haunt him in the form of mycosis fungoides, a rare form of lymphoma caused by excessive exposure to radiation. He suffered from the disease for almost fifteen years before he died in 1945, just shy of his seventy-fourth birthday.[22]

Interestingly, Cannon's obituary appeared in journals of

physiology and anatomy but not in medical journals. While the medical community did not relate his research to theirs, the 164 boxes of his papers housed at the Harvard Medical Library are testament to his role in the development of physiology over the first half of the twentieth century. In the next chapter we will see how Cannon's ideas were advanced by Melvin Page's research into the lifestyle factors that upset homeostasis.

CHAPTER 7

# MELVIN E. PAGE AND BODY CHEMISTRY

*Tell me what you eat, and I will tell you what you are.*
Anthelme Brillat-Savar, Physiologie du gout
(1755-1826)

O nce Walter B. Cannon had set the stage for the study of homeostasis, others began to find applications for his theories. One of these was Melvin E. Page (1894-1983), a dentist who took a very practical approach to helping his patients restore and balance their body chemistry.

## A Dentist's Research

Melvin Page was born in Picture Rocks, Pennsylvania, the eldest of three sons of a physician. He was a middleweight boxing champion during his undergraduate years at Michigan State. After obtaining his Doctor of Dental Surgery degree, he hung out his shingle in Muskegon, Michigan.

Because he had such a large practice, Page soon realized there was a need for better dentures. He set to work and developed dentures based on engineering principles that helped keep the loss of alveolar bone to a minimum. The alveolar bone is the part of the upper and lower jawbone that supports the roots of the teeth. After teeth are lost, the alveolar bone supports the dentures. Although the new dentures were state-of-the-art at the time, many of his patients still had to have them replaced within two and a half years. The jawbones would reabsorb, become smaller, and the dentures would no longer fit. Page wanted to understand why the jaw bone deteriorated and the teeth decayed in the first place. Working at Mercy Hospital and Hackley Hospital in Muskegon, Michigan, he investigated deterioration in the mouths of his patients.[1]

> A dentist has an opportunity to look into the mouths of patients and see a small glimmer of what is going on throughout the entire body.

Page realized that the plaque, decay, and deterioration he saw were all related to other physical problems his patients might be having. To understand why this deterioration was taking place, he studied more than 2,000 hospital patients and his own dental patients' blood chemistries. His studies showed that no bone loss occurred and no cavities formed when blood tests registered the following:

1. There were approximately 10 milligrams per deciliter of calcium in the bloodstream and 4 milligrams of phosphorus. In other words, there was approximately 2.5 times as much calcium as phosphorus in the bloodstream.
2. The fasting blood glucose was close to 85 milligrams per deciliter in the bloodstream.

Page was curious as to what caused the calcium to phosphorus ratio to change. He also wondered why the fasting blood glucose level would deviate from 85 milligrams per deciliter. He found that sugar was the main dietary offender in upsetting the calcium/phosphorus ratio and the body chemistry. Page found that in the presence of excessive sugar, the phosphorus would become depleted. Since minerals only work in relationship to each other, when the phosphorus became depleted, the calcium that was there could not all function. Although the blood might show enough calcium, in the absence of enough phosphorus, the calcium that was there was not all functioning. Therefore, not only was the phosphorus deficient but the functioning calcium become deficient also. The calcium that was there but could not function could become toxic. Since all of the minerals work in relationship to each other, many unusable minerals in the bloodstream can also become toxic and/or deficient. See mineral wheel below.

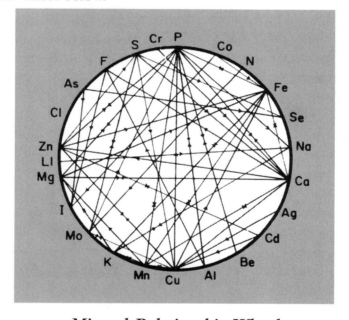

**Mineral-Relationship Wheel**
Dr. Paul Eck, Analytical Research Labs, Phoenix, Arizona

Page found that in a small number of people who ate excessive sugar, the phosphorus would become excessive rather than deficient. This too would upset the delicate mineral balance and make some of the minerals deficient and/or toxic.[2]

> Toxicity in the body is the main reason for disease. The toxicity caused by our abusive live style that makes minerals toxic is the main form of toxicity in the bloodstream, but there are other forms also. Even today most researchers do not realize that minerals only work in relation to each other in an electromagnetic field.

When Page's patients stopped eating sugar, the ratio of calcium to phosphorus was brought close to 10:4, the fasting blood sugar level approached 85 mg, the bones would stop losing calcium, and the tooth decay would decline. Page realized that the degree of tooth decay was in direct proportion to the amount of deviation from the normal fasting blood glucose of 85 milligrams and the normal 2.5:1 ratio of calcium to phosphorus.

Walter Cannon's research was not focused in that direction, but he had also understood the importance of the calcium to phosphorus ratio. In 1929 he referred to "homeostatic agencies that were not considered . . . such as the stabilization of phosphorus in relation to calcium."[3]

Page's professional colleagues must have seen him as a bit of an heretic. He was the youngest man on the staff of either hospital, and his new idea was not accepted. When Page used the approach of balancing the body chemistry with his dental patients, other symptoms would disappear, such as arthritis, headaches, and allergies. This caused him to become unpopular with the doctors. Largely because of their response, Page stopped his research in blood chemistry while he was on staff at the Muskegon hospital.[4]

In 1950, he left his thriving Michigan dental practice for Florida, where he lived for the next forty-three years. He spent his first year as a fisherman because he needed to be a resident for one year before he could get a dental license. He was granted the necessary license, but he never practiced dentistry again. Instead, he became more interested in balancing body chemistry.

At the Page Clinic he started and ran in St. Petersburg,

Melvin Page worked with patients suffering from all sorts of degenerative diseases. Using his knowledge of blood analysis and body chemistry, he helped to prevent and alleviate dental problems in his patients, and he helped them to heal the rest of their bodies as well.

Page had such a high success rate in healing the people who came to his clinic that he was not very popular with the local doctors and dentists. For political reasons, he decided not to accept any local patients, only patients from out of state.

> Melvin Page had retired by the time I was studying at the Page Clinic, and I never met him. I do know many people who knew, admired, and loved him. He did not have much time for nonsense. His no nonsense method of helping people helped them get on with their healing.

Page felt, as Cannon did, that the endocrine system is the main system in the homeostatic mechanisms. The strength of the endocrine system was crucial for optimum physical and mental health. In his 1963 book *Body Chemistry in Health and Disease*, Page wrote:

> The autonomic-endocrine system is the automatic pilot of all the involuntary processes. These processes include respiration, heartbeat, digestion, elimination, the innumerable steps of food use, body temperature control, and many chemical conversions of the utmost delicacy in syntheses, transportation, and assimilation. These are all directed toward the goal of maintaining physical integrity and equilibrium in the individual body.[5]

He came to the realization that all degenerative diseases are the result of malfunctioning endocrine and exocrine glands caused by abusive live style factors.[6] The endocrine glands secrete hormones into the bloodstream—for example, the pancreas secretes insulin to regulate the blood glucose level. The endocrine glands operate as the thermostats, catalysts, and regulators of bodily functions. The exocrine glands, such as the salivary glands, sweat glands and the lacrimal glands, which release tears, secrete onto the body's surface.[7]

Page advocated the same systemic treatment that Cannon used for diabetes, arthritis, and other degenerative diseases that result from the breakdown of some part within the organism. All degenerative diseases, Page found, respond to the same type of systemic treatment as dental cavities.[8] When a part of the body is ill, the whole body is ill. Healing will take place in the whole body. Page felt this was also true of infectious diseases, which he said involved two factors. One of these, a more immediate one, was microbial; the other was the imbalanced body chemistry due to life style factors that allowed the disease to flourish.[9]

Robert Bruce Pacetti, D.D.S. worked at the Page Clinic with Dr. Page. Pacetti came to the Page Clinic as a patient with psoriasis all over his body. Eating the Page diet, Pacetti overcame psoriasis completely. He became so convinced of the Page program that he quit dentistry and worked with Page. Pacetti took Page's research to a far greater understanding than even Page had of his own research and studies. Pacetti was able to determine immediately what a person was doing to upset his or her body chemistry. Pacetti has spent a great deal of his life researching and teaching others the Page method.[10]

After Page died, Tulane University in New Orleans acquired many of the medical records of his patients. Dr. James Brown of the University wrote to many of these patients and sent them questionnaires regarding the state of their health. In their responses, Brown found that most of them felt that as long as they stayed on Page's diet their health was good. See page 143 for Food Plan III, the Page Diet.

> The diet works not because of the nutritional content, but because it does not contain major foods that upset the body chemistry. He found that it is more important what you do not put into your mouth than what you do. His general rule of healing might be stated, "omissions not additions."

## Research into Nutrition

Page's research also showed that certain foods, especially "junk foods," upset the body chemistry and caused the endocrine system to malfunction.[11]

These findings led him to redefine nutrition. Although it is possible to correct someone's diet, he said, the changes don't necessarily correct nutrition. Page found that a person could be eating a good diet, but if a person eats while feeling distress the food will not be able to be metabolized, get into the cells and function at the cellular level. He defined nutrition as supplying the necessary food materials to the body's tissues and cells, and making sure that the nutrients work on a cellular level.[12]

Since the endocrine glands control the assimilation of food, if the glands are not functioning optimally, the body may become malnourished. Even if the digestive system contains the necessary ingredients of good nutrition, the bloodstream, which supplies the ingredients to the tissues, may become deficient in them because of the malfunctioning endocrine system. For example, when a person eats too much sugar, the pancreas can secrete too much or too little insulin. If a person does this consistently, the pancreas can malfunction. These conditions upset body chemistry, and some nutrients cannot get into the cells. When the body chemistry is in balance, the food will get into the cells. Through a diet that does not upset the body chemistry, the calcium/phosphorus ratio and the fasting blood glucose comes back to homeostasis allowing the endocrine glands to heal.[13]

Like Cannon, Page understood that both the endocrine system and the nervous system were important to homeostasis. Cannon was interested in the sympathetic nervous system, but Page was more intrigued by the parasympathetic nervous system. Actions begin in the parasympathetic nervous system by the release of a chemical known as acetylcholine. Parasympathetic nerve fibers slow the heart and initiate intestinal activity (peristalsis). These nerve fibers also help to release fluids from the glands that secrete tears, saliva, and digestive enzymes. They begin the release of bile and insulin, widen some blood vessels, and narrow the pupils, esophagus, and tubes of the lung. They also relax muscles during urination and defecation.

When the body chemistry is upset, either the parasympathetic or sympathetic system may become dominant. Page realized that when the parasympathetic nervous system was dominant, calcium deposits tended to form in various parts of the body. Chronic arthritis, cataracts, or calcium deposits in kidneys, arterial walls, or on the teeth are some problems produced by toxic calcium.

The Standard American Diet (SAD) of refined and devitalized foods causes an upset in the body chemistry and the endocrine glands have to try to adapt to that. The glands then have the difficult task of adapting to the insult while trying to maintain homeostasis. Malnutrition, letting stress become distress in your life, and microorganisms can all play a part in an imbalance as well. The body has the ability to adapt to some junk food, some malnutrition, some negative emotions and some microorganism. When overwhelmed on a daily basis with an overdose of these homeostatic upsetters, the body loses its ability to regain and maintain homeostasis and disease ensues.[14]

The Standard American Diet is often referred to as SAD—and it certainly is!

Page's studies of indigenous people in undeveloped areas showed the effects of the industrially processed foods in the Standard American Diet. Not only Page but Weston Price also traveled to many third worlds. They viewed people in isolated areas of south east Asia, South America, Alaska, and Africa in the 1940s.[15] When these people changed their diet from their native diet to the SAD, it led to structural changes in the bone formation of the body within one generation! Both breathing and chewing could become difficult due to narrowed dental arches. Women could also have difficulty bearing children because of alterations to the structure of the pelvis.[16] Price found evidence that some of the children that changed to the SAD diet developed lower than normal I.Q.s and developed personality disturbances in the form of unsocial traits.[17]

Page believed that those humans whose life style promotes homeostasis live to eighty years and longer. Those whose lifestyle does not promote a balanced body chemistry will not live to be that old. Page was aware that we live in a world that constantly threatens the balanced state that is critical to longevity. He understood that technology has created an artificial environment that can insidiously destroy us all.[18]

> I have found this to be true in my own practice. I have also found that there are very few obese eighty-year-olds. Carrying excess weight puts a stress on the body's ability to maintain homeostasis and reduces life expectancy.

## Conclusions

Through their research, Bernard, Cannon, and Page all added to our understanding of the endocrine system.

Bernard understood the role that the endocrine system played in secreting hormones into the bloodstream to regulate the *milieu intérieur*. He found that endocrine glands transform ingested food into nutrients and store them for future secretion into the bloodstream. These secretions ensure the blood has the chemical composition necessary for health.[19]

Through his studies on hunger, thirst, body temperature, and stress, Cannon realized that the hypothalamus was the main center of control for the endocrine system. Much of his research also dealt with the adrenal gland and the role that adrenaline has in health and disease.

Page found that the endocrine glands control the assimilation of food. Even with a diet of the right foods, if the endocrine glands are not secreting the correct amount of hormones, due to stress and previous poor eating habits, the bloodstream may become both toxic and deficient in nutrients. Page put Bernard's, Cannon's and his own research into practice. When a person removes abusive foods and deals with the stress in his or her life, the calcium/phosphorus ratio and the fasting blood glucose regain homeostasis and the glands start secreting the right amount of hormones.[21] His diet consists of only whole foods, lots of vegetables, small amounts of protein, and small amounts of animal fat. (Read more about this diet in Chapter 12. You can also read about a home test for homeostasis on page 193.)

From the research of Béchamp, Bernard, Cannon, and Page, it is possible to understand that upset body chemistry due to an abusive live style can upset the microzymas, the endocrine system, the immune system, the digestive system, and the nervous system . All these systems play a role in health and disease. In the next chapter we will return to Béchamp's little bodies and to others who have studied subcellular substances in the body.

CHAPTER 8

# OTHER SCIENTISTS WHO VIEWED DISEASE PLEOMORPHICALLY

*More secrets of knowledge have been discovered by plain and neglected men than by men of popular fame. And this is so with good reason. For the men of popular fame are busy on popular matters.*

Roger Bacon (1214-1292)

Many world-class scientists believed in and wrote about pleomorphism. But since Pasteur's germ theory had captured the medical imagination, these scientists were ignored. Little of their work was translated into English or any other language, and most of them died in obscurity. The research of three of these "pleomorphic" scientists could have made a major scientific contribution had their work gained popularity.

## Guenther Enderlein

Guenther Enderlein (1872-1968) was born in Leipzig into a

family of teachers. He studied natural sciences, physics and zoology at the University of Leipzig, Germany, graduating *summa cum laude*. Although he was officially a zoologist, Enderlein was led into serology and bacteriology by the shortage of physicians during World War I. Much of his early education came from the writings of Antoine Béchamp and his concept of pleomorphism.[1]

Enderlein's *Bakterien Cyclogenie (The Life Cycle of Bacteria)* described the microbial world as viewed through his microscope. In precise drawings, he illustrated the developmental phases of bacteria, along with their different structures and special biological functions.[2] He saw that different types of microorganisms flourish in the red blood cells, white blood cells, plasma, and other body fluids. He reasoned that these microorganisms represented an essential part of the life process.[3] In *Bakterien Cyclogenie*, Enderlein explained that when an individual is healthy, the microbes live within the body in a harmonious relationship and help the body's immune system.

In these same media—the red and white blood cells, plasma, and other body fluids—Enderlein also identified disease-causing forms. He believed these tiny, protein-based forms that live in the human blood and body fluids progress within a cycle. Under unhealthy conditions in the body, these life-forms are associated with many chronic diseases.[4]

Enderlein discovered that factors such as poor nutrition, insufficient water intake, stress that becomes distress, the long-term use of antibiotics, hormones, cortisone, and other drugs all upset the body. This, in turn, can provoke severe change or deterioration of the body's internal environment. He also found that the abusive intake of alcohol, nicotine, and other addictive substances can throw the body out of homeostasis. This can lead to a change in the pH value of the blood, tissues, and fluids, causing them to become more acidic or alkaline for extended periods. This unbalanced pH causes the body to become toxic, and the microbes may change into disease-producing forms by passing through more than the normal stages of a specific life-cycle. By attacking the body tissues, these transformed microorganisms can cause illness.

Enderlein called these harmful microbes "endobionts" and the harmful process "dysbiosis," or "a fault in the life process."[5] The endobionts' primal urge is to survive, but they do so at the body's expense. They abandon their duty to sustain the body's integrity in order to assure their own preservation.[6]

Enderlein's research showed that endobionts in a dysbiotic body set up strong defenses that must be broken down before the healing process can begin. The longer the disease infests the body and incubates within it, the more difficult it may be for the body to unblock the defenses and restore itself to health.[7]

The microorganisms can also stay in their natural, primitive, beneficial condition without advancing to higher phases. When they do advance to a disease-causing stage of the cycle, they can either remain in this stage, or they can go back to a healthy stage if the interior environment becomes healthy. The disease-causing stage can be found in most chronic illnesses.[8]

Enderlein discovered that these microorganisms build up through a cycle that could take on countless variations. This led one researcher to label the phenomenon as the "thousand-headed monster" that lives in every person's blood.[9]

Enderlein realized that the human body has physical barriers to foreign invaders, a defense system that provides protection from anything that might hurt us. The skin is the main barrier. It secretes antiseptic substances in the perspiration and the mucous membranes trap foreign matter. The lymph tissues serve as another barrier, guarding the digestive and respiratory tracts. Stomach juices that contain acids to destroy incoming microorganisms also play a role in the defense system. Yet, these barriers do not always defend the body against intrusions.[10]

It is possible to get an infectious disease in one of either two ways. The first is through a toxic terrain, where the body's own cells have pleomorphized from healthy to unhealthy bacteria. The second is through exposure to someone else who is ill. If a sickness lingers for days with sneezes, a cough and runny nose, or if it develops into something more serious, you know that you have a compromised immune system.

Enderlein's discoveries included the finding that the cell is not the primary living unit of the body; rather, there are tiny biological units living within the cells. Contrary to Pasteur, Enderlein did not believe the blood is sterile. He believed it contains microorganisms that, given the proper milieu—or better yet, the improper milieu—can cause illness. He also said that certain microorganisms undergo an exact, scientifically verifiable growth cycle.[11]   Enderlein was a pleomorphist, not a monomorphist, and he explained the difference between those scientists who observed monomorphism and those who believed in pleomorphism.

The possibility of the existence of monomorphism is, as opposed to pleomorphism, based on completely wrong conclusions. The thought process of the old school [monomorphism] is as follows. The many generations of young, one-day-old, pure cultures that monomorphists often work with result in no changes. Therefore, researchers observed no changes. Then, when the monomorphist confronted undeniable variations, he or she thought of impure cultures and flawed research. With this concept, pleomorphism was suppressed, and Pasteur's monomorphs attained absolute mastery.[12]

Enderlein added new information to the study of pleomorphism, but he was not the only one to do so. Another scientist, without a degree other than honorary, built his own microscope and saw sub-cellular structures similar to Béchamp's "little bodies." His name was Royal Raymond Rife.

## Royal Raymond Rife

Royal Raymond Rife (1888-1971) received an honorary Ph.D. degree from the University of Heidelberg, Germany, in 1913. He then studied at Johns Hopkins University in Baltimore.

Rife was trained by the Carl Zeiss Optical Company in Germany. By 1913, he had already developed a microscope that far exceeded others of the day. Then, in 1933, in San Diego, California, he built what he called the "Universal Microscope." This microscope far surpassed the theoretical limitations of the ordinary variety of instruments. The best existing light microscopes could magnify only 1,000 to 2,000 diameters and could view only dead matter.[13] Rife's microscope attained high magnification (50,000 diameters) with an accompanying sharp definition. It allowed the viewer to observe living microorganisms and their movement. Even today, the state-of the-art electron microscope changes the tiny living microorganisms from alive to inert; it puts living microorganisms in a vacuum that induces changes because of a hailstorm of electrons.[14]

Rife used his microscope in his research with Dr. Arthur Kendall, Dean of Northwestern University Medical School and Director of the Northwestern University Research Laboratory in Chicago, Illinois. He also researched and wrote medical journal articles with Dr. Edward C. Rosenow, head of the Department of Research Bacteriology at the Mayo Clinic, Rochester, Minnesota.[15] In publishing his own discoveries at the Mayo Clinic in 1914, Rosenow stated: "Local infections are no longer to be looked upon merely as a place of entrance of bacteria but as a place where conditions are favorable for them to acquire the properties that give them a wide range of affinities for various structures."[16] These various structures are the many changes in form of the unhealthy pleomorphic state.

Using the microscope, Rife and Kendall viewed a culture of B. typhosus bacteria on a free-cell medium. They also saw the poliomyelitis (polio) and scarlet fever microorganisms, which were relatively long, active, and almost colorless. Over time, the two scientists saw these bacilli change, with the appearance of a turquoise-colored granule at one end. Later, in the same culture, they also observed small, oval, free-swimming, turquoise granules. They believed these granules to be the filterable forms of B. typhosus.[17]

Rife viewed the interior of "pinpoint cells" as well as the smaller cells that make up their interior, which are composed of even smaller cells. For every sixteen times the process of magnification and resolution was repeated itself, smaller cells were visible within the smaller cells. His microscope showed a step-by-step journey into the "micro-beyond," revealing the most minute of components.[18]

Over a seven-year period, Rife grew and studied more than 20,000 laboratory cultures of cancer. He concluded that cancer is a virus. Like the viruses of other diseases, they could easily change from one form to another. When he changed the medium on which the microorganisms were growing, the microorganisms changed as well.[19] This is in direct contrast to Pasteur's theory that nothing changes in the body without the presence of an outside invader.

Rife's research showed that all microorganisms fall into one of not more than ten individual groups. If the body becomes unhealthy due to upset body chemistry, the interior environment also becomes unhealthy. This will induce a microorganism from one healthy group to change over into an unhealthy microorganism from that same group.[20] In a toxic environment the microorganisms have no choice. They cannot stay healthy.

He believed the bacteria themselves did not produce the disease. Instead, the disease was caused by the chemical constituents of these microorganisms acting upon the unbalanced cell metabolism of the body. As he said of his experiments with Kendall, "We have often produced all the symptoms of a disease chemically in experimental animals without the inoculation of any virus or bacteria into their tissues."[21]

The human body is chemical in nature. The bacteria that exist normally in the body feed on these chemicals. If the chemicals change as a result of a toxic environment—an unbalanced body chemistry—these same bacteria, or some of them, will also undergo a chemical change.[22]

These bacteria change, usually passing through several stages of growth before they finally emerge as entirely new entities. Rife observed all the stages of growth through the microscope. He saw them go through every stage, from healthy to unhealthy ones.[23]

Observing living microorganisms convinced Rife that germs could not be the cause, but must be the result of disease. Depending on its state, the body can convert a harmless bacterium into a lethal pathogen or disease-producing substance. Under the right conditions of culture, Rife felt, bacteria could metamorphose into small forms that could pass through filters capable of blocking any microbe larger than a virus. Therefore, "filtrationists" was the name given to Rife and others. Orthodox bacteriologists are known as "non-filtrationists" and do not believe that bacteria could change into smaller forms and pass through filters.[24]

Rife saw in the blood of sick people a family of microbes that transformed themselves under various unhealthy conditions into different forms. These microbes transformed through sixteen stages.

Independently, Rife came to the same conclusions that Béchamp, Bernard, Enderlein, and others had reached previously. He could look at the living microorganism through his microscope. He saw that germs arose within the body. They did not cause disease but were the result of disease states.

This discovery, and his subsequent electromagnetically-based cure for cancer and other diseases, unleashed a fury in the microbiological world. *Science* magazine called his microscope a "sensational new instrument."[25] "Is a New Field About to be Opened in the Science of Bacteriology?" speculated an article in *California and Western Medicine* which envisaged a new direction in medicine.[26] The uproar led to Rife's arrest and trial by U.S. medical authorities. The trial proved traumatic to Rife, leading him to a total nervous breakdown and, then, to alcoholism.[27]

In May of 1934, at a Meeting of the Association of American Physicians, Harvard academics Thomas M. Rivers, a virologist, and Hans Zinsser, a professor of bacteriology, were vehement in their criticism of Kendall and the work he had done with Rife. They accused him of introducing the argument of spontaneous generation into bacteriology. The Harvard professors also said they were unable to reproduce the experiments, and that viruses could not grow on a cell-free medium. After that, there were very few discussions of filterable forms. Rife's microscope disappeared and did not reappear until a few decades later, when it was found in pieces in a San Diego garage.[28]

## Wilhelm Reich

While Rife was pursuing his research in the U.S., Wilhelm Reich (1897-1957) was in Europe, studying bacteriology through a different discipline. Reich was born in Bukovina at the eastern edge of the Austro-Hungarian Empire, now Romania. After a tragic childhood, which saw his mother's suicide and the deaths of his father and brother from tuberculosis, Reich fought for Austria in World War One. He resumed his studies in Vienna when the war was over, entering medical school.[29]

Reich was a psychoanalyst by profession, a protégé of

Sigmund Freud, and one of his leading collaborators. But he disagreed with Freud on one key point. Reich believed that mental illness involved both the body and the mind, while Freud maintained that mental illness does not relate to the body. Reich broke away from Freud and the International Psychoanalytic Movement, leaving bitter enemies behind. He entered a field that is known today as biophysics, the study of biological processes by means of the theories and tools of physics.

In January of 1933, Hitler became Chancellor of Germany. Shortly after, the Nazi press condemned Reich as a radical psychiatrist, an anti-Nazi Communist, a womanizer, and a Jew. By 1934, Reich was exiled from central Europe for his radical ideas and went to Norway. He began working on a microscope equipped with lenses that could magnify living microorganisms from 2,000 to 3,000 times their normal size. This was well over twice the magnification achievable with the ordinary microscopes of his day.[30]

With this microscope, Reich saw "vesicles"—minuscule, fluid-containing, bladder-like sacs of a strange blue color. These vesicles appeared in infusions of hay and other substances such as animal tissue, earth, and coal. He saw many of them change when he boiled the preparations, and he concluded that the strange forms were "transitional," lying midway between the realms of life and the lifeless, or the animate and inert. He gave the name "bions" to these elementary stages of life that defy death, and he called the life energy "Orgone." The bions were similar to Béchamp's microzymas and Rife's turquoise bodies.[31]

Reich poured some of his boiled preparations of bions onto a nutrient culture medium. The cultures began to generate peculiar-looking bacteria and amoebae-like forms. It was possible that these bions could have invaded the cultures from the atmosphere, or they could have appeared because he had not properly sterilized the media. To see if the latter was true, Reich heated his bion cultures to a very high temperature, only to find that the ostensibly "dead" mixtures still produced the higher microbial forms.[32]

Another of his experiments dealt with coal particles. He heated coal particles to 1,500 degrees centigrade before immersing them in solution. Classical biologists maintained that no germ could survive above a temperature of 180 degrees centigrade. Still, Reich observed mobile forms from the coal particles immediately after their sterilization.[33]

Reich also studied grass to observe protozoa, the single-celled creatures that are the lowest form of animal life. He put blades of grass in water and left them for fourteen days. When he examined them with a microscope, he saw the cells at the edge gradually disintegrate into vesicles. These eventually broke off from the main structure and floated freely in the water. He described these vesicles as "small bladders, cavities, sacs, cysts, bubbles, or hollow structures."[34] The individual vesicles or particles showed a kind of spontaneous, inner movement. In his view, protozoa developed from the grass disintegrating and forming vesicles, not from the air, as Pasteur had said.[35]

As Pasteur and Béchamp had done, Reich now made infusions of many different types of substances. Sometimes, he would simply allow the substances to disintegrate in water; on other occasions, he would heat them. They would all disintegrate. The bions showed other lifelike characteristics besides pulsation. They moved about and ingested unattached vesicles. They divided into smaller heaps that expanded as they took up fluid or unattached vesicles, thus simulating reproduction and growth. He saw this as the developmental living process that was occurring continuously in nature.[36]

Reich's opponents said his preparations were not completely sterile and there had been accidental infection by "spores" or "germs" from the air. They complained that Reich was observing and culturing known forms of bacteria or protozoal microorganisms, which came from outside. Furthermore, they thought his materials contained spores that were in a dormant state until they were liberated in solution. Other scientists accused him of confusing the new sub-cellular forms he claimed to have discovered with the simple debris that is found in cultures.[37]

Reich countered their objections by sterilizing the substance to be placed in the infusion and the solution. He found that the sterilization procedure not only caused changes to occur, but it appeared more rapidly and caused more rapid movements.[38]

Reich next found that human blood contained microbial bion structures. This finding disputed the doctrine that human blood is sterile, a doctrine that has remained mostly unchanged throughout the world and is still taught in medical schools. During this period in medicine, biology became increasingly attached to physics, which rejected any "mystical" notions as those of a "primal creator" or a "force of life."[39]

This process of bions generating life-forms can be called pleomorphic bacteriology. Could germs appearing in the body be the result rather than the cause of disease, if not always then at least often?

Reich not only understood pleomorphism; he also understood what negative mental attitudes could do to the body. He agreed with Cannon that psychological conflicts were not exclusively in the mind and could spill over to the body. Reich believed that negative emotions develop from the psychological conflict. The residue of the emotions can deposit in the body's muscular structure in the forms of "armoring or layering." These layers can develop into a suit of armor.[40] Today, the basic principle behind "body work" therapy is working with a person's armoring. Treatment modalities such as Rolfing, reflexology, kinesiology, the Alexander Technique, and shiatsu are directed toward removing armoring. All these techniques using body work attempt to release muscular and other tension in the body.

# Conclusions

Working independently, these scientists used a microscope to discover the same small bodies that Béchamp had seen. None of them knew one another, and only Enderlein was aware of Béchamp's research. Even though they were working strictly on their own, they reached similar conclusions. Each of them observed the tiny bodies change from healthy to unhealthy when the environment went from healthy to toxic.

The next chapter will discuss the work of Gaston Naessens, a scientist who is now researching pleomorphism in Canada. When he began his research, he was not aware of these other scientists' discoveries. Now, using a microscope, a camera, and videotape, Naessens has documented the sixteen cycle stages of pleomorphism.

CHAPTER 9

# GASTON NAESSENS AND THE SOMATID THEORY OF DISEASE

*What lies behind us and what lies before us are tiny matters compared to what lies within us.*
Ralph Waldo Emerson (1803-1882)

Gaston Naessens was born in northern France in 1924, the youngest son of a banker who died when Naessens was only eleven years old. As a child, Naessens showed talent as an inventor, building a motorcycle and a mini-airplane. He was pursuing his interest in the sciences, studying physics, chemistry, and biology at the University of Lille, when World War II broke out. Naessens' family was one of many who were moved to southern France as a result of the Nazi occupation. In Nice he received the equivalent of a full university education from professors who had also been displaced from Lille.[1]

Naessens had never heard of Royal Rife or his Universal Microscope, but as a bacteriologist, he was similarly frustrated with the limitations of the conventional microscope. He invented a microscope that could view entities far smaller than those visible through existing light microscopes.[2] His Somatoscope manipulated light and allowed enlargements of 30,000 diameters. It was fifteen times more powerful than the current microscopes, which could only enlarge to 2,000 times, and allowed scientists to view the constituents of human blood in minute detail.[3] As researcher Christopher Bird said of the Somatoscope, "Because it apparently overcomes certain limitations dictated by the accepted laws of optics, its mathematical constants cannot be elucidated in terms acceptable to orthodox science."[4]

State-of-the-art electron microscopes can magnify 100,000 times with a high degree of resolution (150 angstroms). But, as was stated previously, they have one significant disadvantage: they are unable to reveal specimens in their natural living state.[5] The Somatoscope shows somatids alive as they interact and change in the blood.

Naessens observed Béchamp's microzymas through the microscope and called them somatids. They appeared as tiny points of light that moved around in blood samples.[6] He saw microscopic forms far more minuscule than any that had been revealed previously. In the blood of humans, in animals, plants, and rocks there were millions upon millions of these ultramicroscopic, sub-cellular, living and reproducing forms that are critical to existence. When other scientists described these tiny bodies (only in less detail) their findings were dismissed by the scientific community. They were told they were simply seeing specks of dust or other cellular rubbish.

Naessens found that the somatids are indestructible. They resist temperatures of up to 200 degrees centigrade. Even after 50,000 rems of nuclear radiation, acid, and a diamond knife, they still exist. No matter what he tried, Naessens could not kill them. After the death of their host, somatids return to the earth, where they live perhaps eternally. Naessens believes that if there were no somatids, there would be no life.[7]

Naessens also believes somatids are precursors of deoxyribonucleic acid (DNA). They lead to the creation of DNA. Somatids might be the unknown factor between the living and the nonliving. As a group, they contain the hereditary characteristics of each individual. Somatids are electrical in nature; in a liquid milieu, such as blood plasma, one can observe their electrical charge. This charge affects tiny living condensers of energy, the smallest ever found.[8] Naessens believes he has discovered the physical basis for life itself. He also feels he has discovered what is known as the "etheric" body. Without the physical body, which it interpenetrates, this "etheric" body would only be inert matter, as it becomes at death when the soul takes leave of it.[9]

In a healthy body, a body in homeostasis, the somatids go through three normal stages in their life cycle: somatid, spore, and double spore. Naessens studied the somatids in unhealthy people, individuals whose body chemistry was out of homeostasis. He studied the blood of people with rheumatoid arthritis, multiple sclerosis, lupus, candida, and AIDS. He found that, in these people, the somatids not only go through their normal three cycles of life; they go through an additional thirteen cycles, for a total of sixteen. When the somatids go through their sixteen pleomorphic cycles, they change from healthy to unhealthy forms, to bacterial or viral forms that are detrimental to the body. They end their cycles by becoming fungal. These observations convinced Naessens that germs were not the cause of disease, as Pasteur said, but its result.[10]

Without the normal three-stage cycle, cellular division cannot occur, since the cycle produces a special growth hormone that enables such division to take place. French Nobel Laureate Alexis Carrel called this hormone trephone.[11] This growth hormone exists in the bloodstream and allows for a healthy division of somatids.

We have trephone inhibitors in the bloodstream. These inhibitors stop the somatic cycle at the level of the double spore, which is the third cycle. These three cycles are healthy. But when the body is out of homeostasis, it becomes toxic. The trephone inhibitors stop performing in this toxic environment, and the trephone level becomes excessively high. This excess triggers the somatids to continue on to more cycles. Unfortunately, these are not healthy cycles. Naessens believes that the increase in trephones could be due to a deficiency in copper, mercury, or lead.

> This theory corresponds with Melvin Page's research concerning the deficiency of minerals. Page believed that the relationship between the minerals changes when the body becomes upset, and some minerals become deficient. The deficiency did not come about because of a lack of minerals initially, but when the body chemistry is upset, some minerals become depleted, while others become toxic.

Naessens feels that the concentration of inhibitors in the blood may diminish for a variety of reasons, including chronic distress, nutritional deficiencies, chemical abuse, accidents, shock, psychological depression, physical trauma, and other unknown reasons.

> All of the states I have just mentioned can cause upset body chemistry and a body out of homeostasis.

Therefore, the quantity of trephone strongly influences the somatid cycle. The cycle continues its natural (unhealthy) evolution, releasing growth hormones at each stage of the form-changing process. This process begins to disrupt cellular growth, development, and metabolism.[12]

If the level of blood inhibitors is low, or if the trephones are of poor quality, the cycle will continue. The somatids can progress through the sixteen-stage cycle within as little as ninety-two hours. If something is done to restore the blood inhibitors to proper levels, this pathological cycle can stop and return the somatids to healthy ones. In a short time, however, if the inhibitors are not at their correct level, bacteria-like forms, yeast-like forms, mycelium-like forms, and other unusual forms of sub-cellular microorganisms will appear in the blood. The blood receives an abnormal amount of a growth hormone at this time. Therefore, the three healthy somatid cycles are disrupted as the unhealthy sixteen-stage cycle runs its course and, then, repeats itself continually. This destabilization causes cellular development to become seriously compromised. Healthy homeostasis is disrupted, and the end result is a suppressed immune system. Chronic and degenerative diseases take hold and proliferate.[13] The body becomes susceptible to diseases such as AIDS, leukemia, lupus, Epstein-Barr, multiple sclerosis, fibromyalgia, and cancer.

Naessens discovered that bacteria and other microorganisms arise from degenerated sub-cellular components. By studying the blood under his microscope, Naessens was able to link the development of the sixteen-stage cycle with all of these chronic and degenerative diseases. He has pre-diagnosed many diseases long before clinical signs appear following the sixteen stages.[14] Depending on a person's health, the body can allow the trans-formation of harmless bacteria into lethal pathogens. During the thirteen additional and pathological cycles, there is an increased blockage of the immune system, making it less able to remove foreign invaders.

Being able to see somatids in the blood that are beyond the first three stages of the sixteen-stage somatid macrocycle is not necessarily a confirmation of disease. It is an indicator that the cellular level of the organism is developing a disruptive state that will suppress the immune system and open the door to both infectious and degenerative diseases.

Naessens recently discovered that when a patient has a clogged lymphatic system and some somatids are in the six-teenth stage of the cycle, it is a strong indicator of degenerative disease. When the blood contains many somatids in the fifteenth or sixteenth stage in their life cycle, the terminal stages of the somatid cycle, then degenerative disease is a certainty.[15]

## Conclusions

Naessens's research brings pleomorphism and microzymas/somatids to the computer age. With state-of-the-art instruments, it is possible to see and understand the structure and workings of the tiny bodies.

With his microscope and camera, Naessens has videotaped the metamorphosis of the somatid in its successive forms. These pictures are available to the public today.[16] "I've been able to establish a life cycle of forms in the blood that add up to no less than a brand new understanding of the basis of life," Naessens has said. "What we're talking about is an entirely new biology, one out of which has fortunately sprung practical applications of benefit to sick people, even before all of its many theoretical aspects have been sorted out."[17]

> Unfortunately, it does not seem probable that this information will be of interest to the medical community until there is a paradigm shift away from the germ theory.

When people are not in charge of their own health, the ramifications are vast. When it is suggested that disease is caused by something or someone other than the individual, as the germ theory implies, the structure of our whole society is involved on many different levels. In the next chapter we will look at the economic and social consequences of the germ theory, as well as its impact on our health.

CHAPTER 10

# THE CONSEQUENCES OF THE GERM THEORY

*The doctor of the future will give no medicine but will interest his patients in the care of the human frame, in diet, and in the cause and prevention of disease.*

George Bernard Shaw (1856-1960)

When it comes to ideas about health and disease, the germ theory is the newcomer. As we saw earlier, the idea of self-healing has been around for over two thousand years. The germ theory truly has been a curse. Any ideas that challenge its assumptions fall on deaf ears. This has major implications for medical practice, for the provision of health services, directions in research, and education of health care providers and citizens.

Since the germ theory took hold, the development and application of the sciences of nutrition and endocrinology have lagged behind while the pharmaceutical industry has surged ahead. This is primarily because physicians and public health leaders persist in thinking in terms of the germ theory and monomorphism. They do not acquire an understanding of the concept of homeostasis and pleomorphism. Unfortunately, their lack of understanding has economic, social, and medical consequences. Volumes could be written on this subject, but I will only look at information that most directly relates to us as citizens and as health care consumers.

## Health Consequences of Medications

There is no doubt that some medications—antibiotics, in particular—can save lives. Unfortunately, their side effects can vastly diminish the quality of those lives. Many medications suppress the immune system and play havoc with the endocrine glands. Some can cause the lining of the gastrointestinal tract to deteriorate or lead to diseases of the liver. Still others can have negative effects on the heart and circulatory system.[1] A 1998 article in *Time Magazine* showed that more than 100,000 people die each year in hospitals due to an adverse reaction to medication. This is one of the nation's leading killers.[2] Research also shows that more than five million senior citizens use medications that are not appropriate or could cause interactions that lead to hospitalization.

Being hospitalized also puts you at risk in other ways. An estimated five out of every 100,000 hospital patients die of infections they develop while in the hospital. For every 100,000 operations, it is estimated that ten people die of complications associated with anesthesia. And fifty out of every 100,000 people who undergo surgery will die of complications during or after an unnecessary operation.[3]

These statistics are frightening! Now that you know that upset body chemistry causes disease, you will not need to visit a hospital and become one of these statistics.

Probably one of the biggest problems we are facing is the direct result of the indiscriminate use of antibiotics, which has been promoted by doctors and drug companies, and by the general population. People go to the doctor and want a quick fix. And the doctors know that if they do not give those patients a quick fix, they will simply go to another doctor who will provide it. Antibiotics do not differentiate between the harmful and the useful bacteria. They kill off both, to the disadvantage of the gastrointestinal tract, the blood, and the immune system. Within twenty-four hours, one bacterium can multiply to 16,777,220 more bacteria! The more we rely on antibiotics, the greater the likelihood that antibiotics will kill off the weaker microbes, leaving the strongest mutants to survive and reproduce.[4]

> Remember that Pasteur said that a healthy body had no bacteria in it. The body was sterile.

When antibiotics remove healthy bacteria, they leave space for a normal yeast (Candida Albicans) and other strains of yeast to overgrow. In some cases, this overgrowth of yeast can become a significant medical problem. Vaginal yeast infections are not the only result of excessive yeast. Excessive yeast can also cause systemic problems in both men and women. These problems include bloating, allergy-like symptoms after eating, dizziness, headaches, gas, fatigue, and others.[5]

The use of antibiotics in childhood can also result in an increase of chronic diseases later in life. This is not new information. Medical reporter Imago Galdston wrote about the problem as early as 1954, about twenty years after the discovery of Penicillin (1928) and sulfa drugs (1935):

Those whose lives [medicine] has helped to save often face not an extension of existence in well-being and in health, but merely a prolongation of endurance. In the statistical tabulations such individuals appear to have gained years of welcome life, but these may be, and too often prove to be, years of painful travail, years of dependence, unproductive years which in the last analysis are social and individual liabilities rather than assets. . . . Curative medicine in deferring death has indirectly and unwittingly produced a mounting burden of chronic illness. . . . It is calculated that at least one-sixth of our population, 25,000,000 individuals, suffer from chronic diseases. More than half of these are under 45 years of age.[6]

The over-use of antibiotics is also associated with health problems in children. An organization known as the Developmental Delay Registry studies childhood disorders, including autism, speech and language problems, multi-system developmental disorders, skin irritations, sleep disturbances, repetitive behavior, and loss of language. The Registry conducted a nationwide survey of nearly seven hundred children between the ages of one and twelve years. Their study shows a disturbing link between children with developmental delays and high use of antibiotics. Young children who have taken twenty cycles of antibiotics are more than 50 percent more likely to suffer developmental delays. In the United States, the incidence of developmental, behavioral, and mental disorders in children is increasing dramatically. According to conservative estimates, show that the number of children under the age of eighteen with these disorders grew from 4.8 million to 7.5 million between 1990 and 1994.[7]

> The best way to keep children off antibiotics is to remove all junk food from their diet and help them to deal with the stress in their lives.

Drugs other than antibiotics can also cause a variety of problems. A carefully controlled study was conducted with 236 patients recently discharged from a community hospital. These patients had all received three or more prescriptions to treat chronic illness. The study revealed that:

- 88 percent of those in the study had at least one problem as a result of the prescriptions they received;

- 22 percent had at least one potentially serious, life-threatening problem that could have been caused by the prescription medication;

- 59 percent of the patients were given prescriptions for at least one medication which was not the correct drug for the medical diagnosis;

- 28 percent received too high a dose of a drug;

- 48 percent took one or more drugs with harmful reactions;

- 20 percent of the patients received drugs that unnecessarily duplicated the effects of another drug they were taking.[8]

Other research shows that as many as 10 percent of asthma episodes are either induced by other medications or by the drugs intended to control them.[9]

A 1989 article in *Medical Letter* reported a variety of psychiatric symptoms that may develop from a wide range of commonly prescribed medications. These symptoms usually appear when the individual takes a drug and disappear when the drug is stopped. Stopping the drug may lead to withdrawal symptoms; psychosis is one of them.[10]

A review of three thousand arthritis patients by Stanford University researchers showed that those who were taking non-steroidal anti-inflammatory drugs (NSAIDs) were six times more likely to be hospitalized than those who were not. Those who had previous gastric problems were three times more likely to be hospitalized. The researchers believe that NSAIDs have the most serious side effects of any medication widely used in the United States.[11]

There are times when medical doctoring—the allopathic paradigm referred to earlier—can be advantageous. Sometimes a medical condition is advanced and the body's reserves are low. Other times, because of the patient's suffering, life demands, lack of self-discipline, or addictions, natural healing may not work as fast, as effectively, or at all. Allopathic medicine works wonders in crisis medicine, but the decades-long use of drugs can often be more of a disadvantage than an advantage. We have only just begun to identify all the long-term detrimental effects of medications.[12] **Every year new drugs become available— and every year other drugs are taken off the market because their negative, long-term effects have been recognized.**

> I have felt the ill effects, and certainly the long-term ill effects of drugs. I took DES (diethylstilbestrol). In the 1960s and 70s, it was prescribed for women who were supposedly susceptible to miscarry during pregnancy. Thousands of women all over the Western world were given this drug. DES left me more susceptible to cancer, and it left my daughter more susceptible to cancer and infertility.
>
> Although my daughter was unable to give birth herself, the story does have a happy ending. With the use of a surrogate, using my daughter's ovum and her husband's sperm, she became the mother of twins.

## The Health Consequences of Vaccines

There is much conflicting evidence about the efficacy of vaccines. The *Journal of the American Medical Association*[13] and *Drug Safety*[14] agree that vaccines offer many benefits. They also acknowledge that some individuals may have an adverse reaction to vaccines, although they characterize these reactions as mild. Severe problems resulting in permanent damage or death are rare. These medical journals believe that the benefits of preventing the diseases far outweigh the direct risks of vaccination for the individual and the indirect risks to the community. Because so many lifestyle factors can play a role in the disease process, testing the long-term effects of vaccines is difficult.

Béchamp showed that the biological differences between various animal species are sufficiently great to invalidate the theories of immunology. Therefore, research with animals might not necessarily be true with humans. And, of course, every individual is different. When artificial immunity is inflicted upon the body's delicate balance and high organization, the potential for damage is considerable. As we learned in Chapter 5, Béchamp believed that when the microzyma pleomorphize into pathogens, they change into many forms. A vaccine can only affect **one** form during the pleomorphizing cycle. But the microzyma could be in one of ten other stages of the destructive cycle. The vaccine would not affect this different form; nor would it affect any one of the other forms.[15]

There are other reasons why the use of vaccines may cause damage including:

- the vast difference between what goes on in a test tube and what happens in a living body;

- the reaction in an animal model (a horse, guinea pig, or rabbit) is different from the corresponding reaction in humans;

- each individual is different and will react differently to similar environmental changes, including inoculations;

- introducing foreign material into a living organism, even one of the same species, always causes some reaction, most often a toxic one, and sometimes produces serious results.[16]

History shows that even before the use of vaccines, 90 percent of all contagious diseases had been eliminated. This includes whooping cough, diphtheria, tetanus, tuberculosis, cholera, and typhoid. Indoor plumbing, cleaner storage facilities, refrigeration, and more sanitary transportation of food helped to eliminate infectious diseases. Other conditions that helped to remove disease were reduction of famine, the practice of hand-washing before surgery, and the increase in other sanitary living conditions.[17]

> It seems that an unhealthy environment causes disease and epidemics, not by germs.

A study published in *The New England Journal of Medicine* in 1994 showed that more than 80 percent of the children under five years of age who contracted whooping cough had been fully vaccinated. The Center for Disease Control said that the Sabin oral polio vaccine is the only known cause of polio in the U.S. today. The researchers also concluded that the pertussis vaccine failed to give full protection against whooping cough.[18]

## Economic Consequences

Now that you've seen some of the health consequences of the paradigm of the germ theory, let's take a look at what happens in your pocketbook.

Health care is approaching 12 percent of the gross national product.[19] In 1994, the health bill topped one trillion dollars for the first time, up 12.5 percent from the $942.5 billion spent in 1993.[20] Twenty-four cents of every dollar in the U.S. health care system is spent on administration and billing, compared with eleven cents on the dollar in Canada. Between 1980 and 1990, drug prices rose a staggering 152 percent, and drug firms earned a profit of 18 percent on sales of $57 billion in 1990.[21]

Although many infectious diseases have been brought under control, degenerative diseases remain "epidemic." About one out of two people will die of heart disease. One out of three will get cancer. One out of five will develop diabetes.[22] In spite of all the money that is spent on drug research, there are no drugs that will cure these and other degenerative diseases, such as arthritis, osteoporosis, fibromyalgia, environmental illness, or multiple sclerosis.

As for vaccines, the economic consequences of compulsory vaccinations are staggering. Millions of people around the world are vaccinated, and pharmaceutical companies make vast sums of money are a result.

Read your health insurance policy! Most insurance companies do not insure for damages from vaccines. Pharmaceutical companies refuse to accept responsibility for damages from vaccinations. Our government is trying to absorb (with our taxes) lawsuits that, under usual circumstances, could bankrupt vaccine manufacturers, doctors, and hospitals. The federal government started the National Vaccine Injury Compensation Program (VICP), a no-fault system. This agency limits parents to a maximum of $250,000 for the loss of a child. VICP has paid more than $450 million to compensate families for the damage and death caused by vaccines. This money comes from U.S. tax dollars.[23] Does the VICP know something it is not telling parents and the general public?

The misuse of prescriptions costs about $20 billion in avoidable hospital stays. An analysis of Medicare data from 1992 showed that 17.5 percent of the nearly thirty million recipients who were not in hospitals or nursing homes had taken at least one unsuitable drug.[24] One illustration of the incredible sum of money that is spent on a single medication is amoxicillin, one of the drugs most commonly prescribed for infants and children with ear infections. In 1994, consumers spent $70 million on amoxicillin.[25] How much of this money was spent unnecessarily?

Here is another example. The American Heart Association estimated that the cost of cardiovascular disease in 1992 was $108.9 billion. Cardiovascular disease accounted for approximately 44 percent of all deaths in the United States.[26] There is no doubt that many of those deaths were directly related to lifestyle issues such as diet, smoking, obesity, lack of exercise, stress, and so forth.

To get an average estimate of the cost, a study tracked coronary artery disease patients for five years from the time of diagnosis until death. The average estimated five-year cost was as follows: acute myocardial infarction, $51,211; angina pectoris, $24,980; unstable angina pectoris, $40,581; sudden death, $9,078; and non-sudden death, $26,916.[27] These are only the economic costs to the health care system. They do not take in the human costs, such as the loss of quality of life.

Blue Cross, Blue Shield, and Medicare will pay $30,000 for a coronary bypass operation and more than $100,000 for a heart transplant. But many insurance companies will not pay $1,000 to $2,000 for various cardiac rehabilitation programs.[28] Nor will they pay for chelation therapy, an alternative therapy that is used successfully for many patients with coronary heart problems and is certainly more cost-effective that surgery.

## Help Is On The Way

Many large companies have been looking for ways to reduce health care costs. Coors developed a wellness facility that deals with health risk assessment, nutritional counseling, stress management, smoking cessation, weight loss, blood pressure screening, family counseling, and prenatal and postnatal education. This wellness and fitness center saves the company an estimated $1.9 million annually. For every dollar Coors spent on this program, they saved an estimated $6.15 from decreased medical costs.

Another company, Tenneco, Inc., evaluated the benefits of a supervised exercise program. They found that those employees who exercised had fewer sick hours per year than those who did not (forty-seven hours versus sixty-nine). Employees who did not exercise had average medical care costs that were almost twice as much as those who did. In female employees, this difference was even greater.[29]

Victor Penzer, M.D., wrote to the CEOs of several insurance companies describing a logical way for them to save money and reduce human morbidity and mortality. He received no reply. Then he happened to speak to an insurance executive about his idea. The executive told him that if Penzer thought the insurance industry would be interested in saving petty sums by paying less in benefits, he may be right—but only to a point. He went on to say that insurance companies will deny benefit payments whenever they can get away with it, but this is not where insurance companies make their money. In the CEO's words:

> Should the mortality and morbidity rates drop, we would be forced to raise our premiums. Our income is made not on marginal benefit savings, and not even on the premiums themselves. The premiums are merely the vehicle for getting hold of significant funds for investments in the financial market. That's where real money can be made. If the mortality and morbidity rates would drop, premiums would be forced down, we would have less money to invest and, hence, smaller profits.[30]

"These," according to this executive, "are the economic facts of life."

## Why the Problem?

Dr. Parker Griffith, of the Huntsville Cancer Center, believes that the health care bureaucracy that exists in the medical-industrial complex is not necessarily attributable to one sector. This bureaucracy developed a whole process and a system. Griffith does not believe it is necessarily calculated to do so, but it is interfering with the development and marketing of new therapies for cancer and other diseases.[31] He believes the interference occurs because directions in research are dictated by pharmaceutical companies. He is not sure whether the problem is due to a global plot designed to protect the pharmaceutical companies, or if it is just a sticky mess of bureaucratic machinery that grinds very slowly. As Griffith says:

> In my particular view, patients who are ill with the disease, which physicians know is going to take their lives, are still subjected to routine, common, and unworkable solutions that continue to be applied without any thought of any trials of new things developed by investigators who may not be a part of the accepted medical community.[32]

On one hand, Griffith says, our system attacks innovative programs, and doctors are afraid of "taking a chance," because of lawsuits, insurance premiums, and other economic factors. On the other hand, doctors do not want to put patients in a life-threatening situation by giving them drugs that have not been adequately tested. Drugs that were new in 1990 did not get into doctors' offices until 1996 or 1997.

We may select only "the best and the brightest" to study medicine, but within a short time these doctors get caught in the financial-political system. Griffith does not believe the American Medical Association (AMA) is very innovative. It did not bring the first lawsuit against the tobacco companies; nor did it pioneer nutritional information. Of the 780,000 doctors in the U.S., only 250,000 are members of the AMA.[33] The association does not represent and speak for all the doctors. It is a trade association, just like the Trial Lawyers' Association or other professional groups with vested interests and a status quo to protect.

As I mentioned earlier, cancer is on the rise in the United States, not only in the aging population but in increasingly younger people as well. The scientific community needs new information. Multi-billions of dollars are spent on the treatment of cancer, but only a tiny fraction of that is spent on early diagnosis, prevention, or on the question of what causes cancer in the first place. The idea of stimulating the immune system so that it can identify malignant cells and destroy them would be one suggestion for preventing cancer. Griffith concludes that the whole health system has the problems it is having today because of habit, tradition, economic pressure, and a lack of innovative spirit.[34]

> Speaking of medical school, few medical schools in the United States have required classes in nutrition. If classes are given, they are few in number. Nurses learn more about nutrition than doctors do.

Carl Menninger would agree. After twenty-five years as a psychiatrist, he believed that the accepted formula for diagnosing and treating a patient rarely worked. The procedure is to collect data about a patient, organize the data, establish a diagnosis, and treat the patient according to that diagnosis. Menninger concluded that this formula was inaccurate, misleading, and philosophically incorrect.

Medical school had taught him that the world was full of healthy human beings. The few who were struck by an infestation, a lurking bacterium, or a malignant cell—they were the only unhealthy people. Menninger said he hadn't realized how much of our own suffering we determine, want, and even inflict upon ourselves. It seemed to him that the most logical treatments often made people worse instead of better.

Menninger realized that clinicians needed to think of disease as a disturbance in the total economics of the personality. He believed disease occurred when the organism's efforts to maintain a continuous internal and external adaptation were temporarily overwhelmed. This was the result of continuously changing relationships, threats, pressures, instinctual needs, and reality demands. It is the imbalance that is the real pathology. Disease is an imbalance that threatens the comfort or survival of the individual.

Menninger believed Cannon's concept of biochemical homeostasis needed to be extended to encompass an understanding of psychological and sociological homeostasis, which contributed to the total personality. As Menninger said, "The thoughts, feelings, behavior and social relationships of patients, no less than their tissues and their body fluids, follow the same principle, the principle of continuous adaptive shifts and reciprocal balances."[35] He believed that, in the future, one medical discipline should not be able to diagnose disease. Menninger wrote this almost fifty years ago. Few took heed, and yet the Menninger Clinic, one of the most famous clinics in the United States, is named in his honor.

## Conclusions

The germ theory has taken responsibility away from the individual and handed it over to the medical community and to society. As a result, the scientific community has lacked a broad direction in looking at the cause of disease. These are some of the reasons why research has been hindered:

- Pharmaceutical companies direct most of the research that is going on.
- The government moves slowly to introduce new medicines, to regulate those that are already on the market, and to remove those that are destructive.
- Few from outside the medical community are able to introduce new ideas.
- Routine and unworkable ideas continue to be used.
- Lawsuits, insurance company restrictions, and other economic factors restrict innovative ideas.
- Doctors do not think in terms of what a patient is doing to cause his or her disease.
- Patients are given little responsibility—or control—in the treatment of their own disease.

If these trends continue, the cost of medicine will continue to rise, and the rates of degenerative diseases will continue to increase. As consumers, we will become less satisfied with the medical profession. Health, social, and economic problems related to health will escalate.

Enough people have suffered. It is now time for the medical paradigm to shift to a more holistic approach that uses the teachings of Bernard, Béchamp, and Cannon.[36] This approach deals with the new word—"psycho-neuro-endocrino-gastro-immunology." The next chapter will explain how we can all become responsible for our own health.

## A Global Problem

In parts of Asia, Africa, China, Russia, and South America where the people eat their native foods and do not live in polluted societies, infectious diseases still abound. Malaria, pneumonia and other chest diseases, gastrointestinal diseases, tuberculosis, and AIDS are major problems. Most of these diseases are due to poor sanitary living conditions: no refrigeration, no indoor plumbing, and polluted water.

But in these same societies, degenerative diseases such as heart disease, cancer (except as it relates to AIDS), allergies, arthritis, multiple sclerosis, diabetes, osteoporosis, or others are rare or unknown.[37]

I just came back from Southeast Asia. While traveling on the island of Penang in Malaysia, I was struck by what was happening in terms of "growth." Until very recently, this country was a primitive country with few of our modern degenerative diseases. The main city of Georgetown has had incredible development and now has many, many skyscrapers. The community was building two new hospitals. A new medical complex, the Chua Medical Center, advertises itself as a "Public Specialist Center." One office was devoted to plastic and cosmetic surgery; another was for an eye, ear, and nose specialist; a third was for a hearing specialist. Across the street was a "7-11," with all the same junk food you can buy in any convenience store in the United States. Down the street was an exercise facility. The people need this facility because they no longer wash their own clothes, churn

*continued*

butter, walk to school or to work. They do not get exercise as part of their daily life.

What is happening in Penang is happening all over the world. I have had the opportunity to travel to many Third World countries. I have been in villages in China, Zimbabwe, and Papua New Guinea. I have been in areas where there is no plumbing, no electricity, and the only water comes from the stream or river. Health officials in these areas all say the same thing. As long as native people stay in their villages, degenerative diseases do not occur. If they go to the cities, the diseases become a part of their lives. The city lifestyle of processed foods and junk food, stressful living conditions, and environmental pollution takes its toll on their health. Most people do not understand this. Even if they do understand, most of them are not willing to go back to their villages. The city life holds so much more excitement and adventure.

Unfortunately, I do not see a short or a long-term answer. These people will have to go through exactly what we are going through. Degenerative disease will skyrocket in these areas. Infectious diseases are still a huge problem in developing countries. These people will have to deal with both infectious diseases and degenerative diseases.

It saddened me to see these developing nations wanting so much of what we have—and getting it. Some of what they want is the worst of what we have. If they were to stay in their native villages, improve sanitary conditions, work toward indoor plumbing and electricity, better their education system, and continue to eat their native foods, they could bring the best of our advances in agriculture and computer technology to their community. And they would be far better off.

CHAPTER 11

# LIFTING THE CURSE OF LOUIS PASTEUR

*For new ideas to be accepted, one has to wait for a generation of scientists to die off and a new one to replace it.*

Max Planck (1858-1947)
Nobel Laureate in physics, 1918

In his book, *Cross Currents*, science writer Robert Becker characterizes the current medical paradigm as follows:

It is based on the chemical-mechanistic concept of life. In this view, living things are chemical-mechanistic machines whose capabilities are restricted to those functions permitted by this model. There is no place for any characteristics, such as autonomy of self-healing, that do not fit the mold. This view was reinforced until it became a dogma, the proponents of which claimed to know everything there was to know about life. This paradigm not only dominates our society but rules the medical profession as well, limiting both the methods that could be used to bring about a cure and our perception of the ability of the human body to heal itself.[1]

How do we move beyond a paradigm that is holding back the progress of medical science and affecting the health of millions of people?

To replace any paradigm requires a revolution of sorts. In the case of science, as philosopher Thomas Kuhn points out in his classic book *The Structure of the Scientific Revolutions,* "normal" science—the "ruling scientific outlooks" which dominate any given period in history—will only change in favor of a more novel approach. For this to happen, the time must be ripe.[2] The proposal of a new paradigm is premature if a series of simple logical steps cannot connect all the ideas that might lead to a new medical paradigm.

The time is now ripe for a change from the paradigm of the germ theory—as you have seen in these pages. The first logical steps toward the creation of a new model have already been taken. This is self-evident by all the people who are still in pain and sick and going to alternative doctors seeking answers.

## The current paradigm of the germ theory is based on questionable assumptions.

Most textbooks teach monomorphism, the notion that the microbe is all-powerful and the host organism is a passive victim.[3] The evidence is now there to show that this information needs updating. Late twentieth-century bacteriology has lost confidence in the "fixity" of microbial species.[4] Today, many bacteriologists admit there are no fixed species. Even in highly controlled, artificial laboratory environments, bacteria will change both form and function quite readily. Fixed, typical cultures are difficult to maintain.[5]

Although their research has largely been ignored, for over a century, scientists have been studying and have understood the concept of pleomorphism, that bacteria are form-changing or pleomorphic. Their research has shown that when placed in a body that has been made toxic by a diet of highly processed "junk" foods, bacteria can metamorphose into forms small enough to pass through filters.[6] These scientists are referred to as "filtrationists." The allopathic medical community has not acknowledged pleomorphism. It continues to believe in the non-filtrationist microbiologists' theory of monomorphism. Now that it is possible to view these pleomorphic changes through a camera, it is hard to ignore the filtrationists' views.

Pleomorphism implies that the body is an active participant in infection and disease. It means that we can create our own disease. If our diet includes many junk and processed foods, we can change the healthy elements that live in our body into unhealthy ones. This new avenue of thinking will help scientists to search for a more broadly based cause of disease.

## The concept of the body as a self-regulating mechanism— a body in homeostasis—is becoming mainstream.

The concept of monomorphism essentially wiped the slate clean of most of the teachings that had been around since early history, including the notion of self-healing and the natural equilibrium of the body. Thanks to the groundbreaking work of Walter B. Cannon and to the new field of psychoneuroimmunology, which is now researching many of Cannon's discoveries from close to a century ago, homeostasis is being recognized as critical to health. While Cannon's work has been largely ignored by the medical community, much of what he discovered about homeostasis is now finding its way into current teaching about health. *Human Development and Homeostasis* is even the title of a college science textbook.[7]

Since disease can be viewed as any persistent, harmful disturbance of the equilibrium of many body systems, a more complete, holistic study of disease would be psycho-neuro-endocrino-gastro-immunology.[8] Any more broadly based study of disease must include the two critical areas of medicine that Cannon and Melvin E. Page studied extensively: endocrinology and gastroenterology.

**Living conditions, not germs, may be the determinants of health or disease.**[9]

We now understand that the infectious disease epidemics that used to be commonplace occurred because people were living cheek by jowl in poor sanitary conditions and without the technological advantages we now enjoy. In the United States, most of us now have running water, indoor plumbing, and refrigeration to prevent our food from being spoiled. We are fortunate to live in circumstances where infectious diseases are less likely to gain a toehold than they are in the developing world.

However, despite the incredible time, money, and intellectual brain power that is being spent on medical research, infectious diseases are on the rise in the U.S., and the incidence of degenerative diseases is increasing as well. This is because all of that time, energy, and money has been spent looking for the cure for disease rather than at the cause—the way we live today. This includes the processed food, the chemicals, the polluted water and air, the lack of exercise, and the daily distress that encompasses many of our lives. All the research showing the detrimental effect of many junk and processed foods is available, but the government and the medical community, as well as average citizens, are choosing to ignore it.

**The paradigm of alternative medicine is not the answer.**

The alternative medicine community is bringing on a new paradigm, showing that, in many instances, natural healing can replace allopathic medicine with very few side effects. But medically trained people, whether they are in the allopathic or holistic field, usually look for a remedy rather than a cause.

In late 1992, Congress established the Office of Alternative Medicine (OAM) within the Office of the Director, National Institutes of Health (NIH) to "facilitate the fair, scientific evaluation of alternative therapies that could improve many people's health and well-being." The six fields of alternative medicine that fall under the OAM's umbrella include: mind\body (studying bioelectromagnetics); alternative medical practices (traditional Oriental medicine, acupuncture, homeopathic, environmental medicine, and others); manual healing therapies (osteopathic, chiropractic, and massage therapies); pharmacological and biological treatment (chelation and biologically guided chemotherapy); herbal medicine, and diet and nutrition, with an emphasis on studies involving megadoses of supplements.[10]

Look closely at this list and you will see the influence of the medical paradigm of the germ theory. Most of these are treatment modalities involving natural remedies. Few of them deal with the cause because few think in these terms. The alternative medical community is bringing on a new paradigm, showing that natural healing can replace allopathic medicine in many instances with very few side effects. But all allopathic and alternative therapies should be looking for causes, not treating symptoms.

Instead of continuing to explore treatments that are directed at cure rather than cause, I believe it would be beneficial to add the following goal to the OAM's fields of study: Increase awareness and understanding of homeostasis and pleomorphism through the research of Bernard, Béchamp, Cannon, Page, Enderlein, Rife, Reich, Naessens, and others.

**The responsibility for health must be returned to the individual.**

The idea that a doctor will take care of us has become part of our notion of staying healthy. Too many of us gladly surrender responsibility for our health to a physician we believe is a miracle worker in a white coat.

"What are you doing to cause your own illness?" is the first question doctors should be asking us. Instead, they ask "What are your symptoms?" Alleviating those symptoms then becomes a matter of prescribing a pill, which will often mask the real problem.

## Making the Change

With degenerative diseases and infectious diseases on the rise, it is definitely time for a medical paradigm shift. Like any paradigm shift, this one will take time and a big push. It will also lead to huge changes in a system that is skewed towards illness rather than health.

The change must start with the doctors. The medical community must be willing to work with and learn from anyone who can help to improve a serious health problem.

Another shift must come from all of us as patients. We must be willing to make what are sometimes dramatic lifestyle changes rather than take pills. Some of these changes will not be easy. Substituting new eating patterns for old, making the time to exercise regularly, and not letting stress become distress all involve discipline and effort. Most people find these changes very difficult to make.

Our approach to consumer health education must change as well. Much of health education consists of telling the public about their chances of falling victims to this or that disease and warning them about the symptoms of those diseases. Very little time is devoted to teaching youngsters— or even adults!—to understand their body's symptoms and to take charge of their own health.

And we must change the way our doctors are educated at medical schools, shifting the emphasis away from the study of remedies for diseases to lifestyle factors that could be causing disease. Doctors and health practitioners must acquire the skills to teach people how to take care of themselves rather than take pills. They must learn to ask that all-important question: "What are you doing to cause your own illness?"

## The Impact of Change

Any change of this magnitude will have an impact on all areas that are touched by the medical system. The impact on pharmaceutical companies would be considerable, since so many of the drugs manufactured today are designed to manage symptoms. Most drugs are not necessary when a body has healed and is in homeostasis. People will die of natural causes rather than of the diseases that claim their lives today. They will live longer but without disease, and they will be able to die at home. This would, of course, affect many hospitals and nursing homes.

Some insurance companies have already started paying for preventive medicine as well as curative medicine. Many of them have increased premium rates for smokers. Soon they will realize that the costs of carrying clients with other unhealthy lifestyle habits is also high. This could lead to increased premiums for people who are obese, take street drugs, abuse alcohol, eat junk food, and do not exercise regularly.

When the ill effects of much of our diet become known and people eat more non-processed and less harmful food, food manufacturers will need to divert their unhealthful products to much more healthful products, or divert the manufacturing to non-food items.

## Lifting the Curse of Louis Pasteur

Louis Pasteur's germ theory has, indeed, been a curse. But I believe that if we take responsibility for our own health, that curse can be lifted.

Still, the writing is on the wall. Unless we change our lifestyle, there will be no change in those alarming statistics I spelled out in the first chapter. In fact, they will probably get worse. Unfortunately, that may be just what it will take before the message gets across—more of us having more symptoms, more sickness, and more pain before we finally say to ourselves, "Hey, what is going on here? This has to stop!"

That's where you are right now in this book. You understand what really causes disease. The next section will give you the information and the courage you need to realize, "Hey, I can stop it!"

CHAPTER 12

# OUR PRESENT AND FUTURE PATH

Now that you understand the problem, you will be able to solve it. Put your body back in homeostasis and it will heal. Let the body only go through three healthy stages of pleomorphism rather than eleven unhealthy stages.

Listen to what your body is telling you. Heed symptoms such as headaches, falling asleep after meals, joint pains, bloating, allergies, high blood pressure, yeast infections, chronic fatigue, diarrhea, constipation, gas, skin problems, swelling, or a full-blown degenerative disease. If you believe these symptoms come out of the air, then you are under the curse of Louis Pasteur. You have given responsibility for your life to others. But if you realize that you are doing something yourself to cause these symptoms, you know you can do something to stop them.

From reading this book, you now understand that the body can become toxic when you upset its body chemistry. The toxicity can come from the bacteria in your body pleomorphizing and changing from healthy to unhealthy bacteria. That is definitely toxicity in the body.

There are other ways the body can become toxic. Briefly, when you upset your body chemistry, some of the minerals become excessive and can become toxic. So toxic minerals are another form of toxicity in the body. Other minerals become deficient. When the minerals become deficient, the enzymes will not function properly, because each of those many enzymes is dependent upon a mineral to function. Since enzymes help us to digest our food, the food will not be digested or metabolized properly because of the lack of enzymes. The result is particles of improperly digested food in the bloodstream. When the immune system encounters these microscopic particles, it does what it would do with any other "invader." It produces antibodies to get rid of the partially digested foods. This is one form of food allergy, partially digested food in the bloodstream.

Although it is the immune system's job to deal with foreign invaders, it was not designed to come to our defense in this way, meal after meal, day after day, year after year, over decades. It becomes exhausted by this pattern and it cannot respond appropriately to more serious invaders. The body becomes increasingly susceptible to infectious and degenerative diseases. What disease we will get as a result depends on our own genetic blueprint.

You can reverse this disease process! Disease is toxicity in the body, in the bloodstream. The healthy bacteria that pleomorphize to unhealthy bacteria are toxicity. Toxic minerals and partially digested food are toxicity. When the body is put back in homeostasis, back in balance, the immune system will free the body of toxicity. Stop doing to your body what you did to make it sick, and it will heal itself. For more information on body chemistry, read my book *The Secrets of Natural Healing with Food*.

The quality of your health depends on the harmony of your body's electrochemical balance, the measurable electrochemical condition within and around your body. Your life actions in four key arenas will determine if your electrochemistry stays in balance, in homeostasis.

The following four primary life actions either enhance or upset electrochemical balance.

- **Arena I** involves the choices we make and how we interpret what we and others do, think and say.

- **Arena II** deals with what we put in our mouths, whether that is food, water, alcohol, cigarettes or tobacco products, pharmaceuticals or street drugs.

- **Arena III** deals with our environment, our sources of light, heat, and electricity, microwave ovens, the chemicals in our homes, the mercury amalgam fillings in our teeth, and aluminum. This arena also includes our body habits, such as exercise, toilet habits, sleep and rest.

- **Arena IV** includes our physical structure, the alignment of our bodies.

Let's take a closer look at these four arenas one by one.

## Arena I

Doctors are rethinking medicine's time-honored tenets that the mind and body are distinct and separate entities. There definitely is a body-mind connection. In fact, it seems to be a two-way street. What we ingest can affect our mind, and what we think, feel, and say can affect our body. Many times our head gets in the way of our body's getting well. Our body is a stimulus response mechanism. It can only respond to whatever happens to it. This response is not right or wrong, good or bad. It is simply the only response the body can give. If you are angry when you eat, your body will respond one way. If you are happy when you eat, it will respond in another way. It has no choice.

Let me give you an example of how a situation will enhance or upset your body chemistry. If someone is angry and yells at you, you have a few choices as to how you will react. You can take it personally and complain. You can internalize it and say nothing. You can get angry and yell back. None of these responses will enhance your body chemistry.

The best way to deal with this situation is to decide that it is not your problem. It is the other person's problem. It is very difficult when you go to someone in anger, or when someone comes to you in anger. It is a put-off. But anger is not usually the issue here. Anger covers up the pain one is feeling. So tell the other person about that pain rather than about the anger. It is also easier for another person to hear about your pain than to listen to you talk about your anger.

If you do become distressed by anger, depression, rage or holding judgments against others, then I suggest you do not eat when you feel this way. Under those conditions, it will be difficult for your body to digest the food you eat. Do something else instead. Get some exercise, run, breathe deeply, listen to a relaxation tape, meditate—do anything to take the stress off your body. To paraphrase the writer Mark Bradford, "The person who eats beer and franks with cheer and thanks will probably be healthier than the person who eats sprouts and bread with doubts and dread." The psychological aspect of health is just as important, if not more important, than the nutritional aspect of health. Both can contribute to upset body chemistry.

There are many things you can do to reduce stress that don't involve quitting your job or divorcing your spouse. Scores of books offer advice on the subject. There are also many cassette tapes available that you can listen to in your own home. Check your local library to see what they have on their shelves. Many stores that sell cassette tapes also have catalogues listing titles and will order them for you.

Watch the newspaper for weekend workshops on stress management. These can be the beginnings of exploration about how to deal with the stress in your life.

Remember there are also many good counselors who specialize in helping their clients cope with stress. Ask for recommendations from friends or organizations that offer programs in stress management.

As Norman Cousins suggests in his book *Anatomy of an Illness*, it is possible to harness the healing powers of the mind. Studies show that life's stresses, such as the death of a loved one, marital break-up, or severe depression can impair immune system function. How we handle these stressful events is the most important factor in determining whether we will suffer ill effects as a result of the stress.

There is interesting research that shows exactly what stress can do—and does not have to do!—to the body. One researcher conducted a study involving heavy smokers and stress. He found there was no difference between the number of stressful events (such as marriage problems, death, etc.) his subjects experienced. However, the research showed that those smokers who developed lung cancer perceived these stressful events as more negative than those smokers who did not develop the disease. They also felt more guilty about them than those smokers who did not develop the cancer.

This takes us back to the question I asked in Chapter 2. Why is it that some people rarely get sick and when they do, they get well rapidly? I think we can learn from these people, since these self-healers have a few things in common. They view life as a challenge rather than as a threat. They live life to the fullest. Self-healers also seem to share a feeling of being in control of their lives.

There are two types of self-healers who recover quickly from illness. The first are extroverts who seek out stimulation, are spontaneous and fun-loving. The second are active and involved, but also calm and bemused. Although they, too, enjoy the company of others, these people choose to have only a few close friends. The self-healing personality has an exuberance that infects others. The core of their good health is positive emotions. They have a sense of choice in life, a commitment to higher goals, an attitude of social integration, and a sense of creative self-fulfillment.

As far as I am concerned, life is very exciting. There are so many things that I want to do! I want to see the world—every corner of it. I want to tell people what I know about health because it is very painful to watch people go through life in physical and/or mental pain when it is not necessary.

I have at least eighteen books I want to read. Someday I am going to learn how to do off-loom weaving. I'd like to take a class in cultural geography. My list goes on. I hope that you are also excited about the possibilities out there. They are endless. And that excitement for life is one of the key factors in good health.

## Arena II

Healthy food can enhance body chemistry, and unhealthy, "abusive" food can upset it. Having a positive attitude will help the body to heal more easily; similarly, the food that you eat—or rather the food that you don't eat!—will help your body to heal.

Foods such as sugar, fried foods, rancid fats, over-cooked food, over-processed foods, alcohol, and caffeine can all upset body chemistry. Foods that allow the body to heal are vegetables, grains (for many people this does not include wheat), beans, and small amounts of protein. Fruits are healthy foods for healthy people, but if you are unhealthy you may need to remove all simple sugars from your diet for a period of two months to allow your pancreas to heal.

Remember, what you do **not** eat is often more important than what you do eat. You could have a perfect meal of a salad, brown rice, vegetables and a form of protein. But if you follow it up with a dessert of pumpkin pie made with sugar, honey or concentrated fruit juice, the fructose and glucose in those simple sugars will upset your body chemistry. You won't get the nutrients from the salad, rice, vegetables and protein. The answer is to go back to God's food. God made food for health.

Don't eat man's food. Man made food for profit, shelf life, and consumer appeal.

Make sure you drink enough water to stay hydrated. Fruits and vegetables are mostly made up of liquid. If you eat a lot of fruits and vegetables, you will already be getting plenty of liquid. Most people should have the equivalent of six glasses of liquid a day. If you are very physically active, you will need more.

With any type of illness, you have upset body chemistry. Your body is out of homeostasis. You will need more rest. Slow down, sleep more, and give your body a chance to rest and heal. No doubt you've heard the old saying "Feed a cold and starve a fever." I don't believe it. As far as I'm concerned, it should be "Starve a cold and starve a fever." Because your minerals will be upset and your enzymes will not be able to function as well, it is better not to eat very much when you're sick. Just eat a little bit. You may prefer to drink broths or purée your food. Eat small amounts during the day and drink lots of water. If you are drinking fruit juices, drink small amounts, possibly watered down, and drink them alone. It would be wiser to drink vegetable juice, which does not have much sugar.

Any food you eat is not going to digest as well when you are sick. You may become allergic to that food. When you are sick and you eat, you could get abdominal symptoms or any other symptoms. You might rotate your foods so that you are not eating the same food more than once every two or three days. You might also want to try some digestive enzymes. Remember that this upset is only temporary. When you regain your health, you will find that the food that did not agree with you while you were sick no longer upsets your stomach. When your body is balanced, the food will be easily digested. Don't forget at all times to chew, chew, chew your food. Digestion begins in the mouth.

Arena II also includes other things you put in your mouth, such as prescription and over-the-counter medications.

Although prescription drugs are life-savers and are beneficial on a short-term basis, the long-term use of them can continually upset body chemistry, leading to degeneration. This is also true of many over-the-counter drugs. Take as few pharmaceutical and over-the-counter drugs as possible, and even then, take them only on the advice and consent of a physician. *Johns Hopkins Medical Letter* wrote that 125,000 Americans die each year as a result of their pharmaceutical prescriptions. In 1989, the General Accounting Office released findings indicating that 51.5 percent of all drugs approved from 1976 through 1985 by the Federal Drug Administration (the FDA) carried "serious post-approval risk." The report revealed a virtually non-existent post-approval drug review procedure. There are many types of drugs that continually are taken off the market due to the long-term effects. New ones appear and, after a few years, they too are taken off the market.

## Arena III

Research shows that classical and new age music enhances body chemistry. Hard rock music causes the body chemistry to become upset. While you are eating, you might listen to slow, melodic music. Harmonious music not only helps in digestion, but research also shows that it helps you to eat less.

Exercise helps to balance the body chemistry. This exercise should include some form of stretching, weight-lifting, and aerobics. The best aerobic exercise is exercise that balances and centers the body, such as walking, jogging, running, tennis, aerobics, dancing or the Rebounder™. If you do not get regular aerobic exercise, remember to breathe deeply eight or ten times a day. Exercise is great for maintaining cardiovascular vitality, preventing osteoporosis, reducing stress, and controlling blood sugar levels. Besides, it can be just plain fun! Find something you like to do and do it.

Toilet habits are important. When nature calls, answer or

nature might stop calling. Our bodies want to get rid of their waste products. If you squeeze the anus and don't go to the toilet, you force the body to retain endols, cadaverines and other putrefaction by-products. Then the immune system has to deal with the by-products. If you are already compromising your immune system, it can become exhausted.

We need rest. Sleep at least six hours a night. An over-worked body becomes distressed, which upsets the body chemistry. Even if you love your work, you can become over-worked with unhealthy results. There is a time for work and play.

It is also important to avoid becoming chilled or overheated. Both hyperthermia and hypothermia can upset the body chemistry. If you are in extreme temperatures, whether they are too cold or too hot, you will be vulnerable to whatever disease-causing bacteria or virus is around.

Use as few chemicals as possible in your home. There are many alternatives that are natural products available in health food stores and via mail-order catalogs. Dry clean only those garments that absolutely can't be laundered. Perchloroethylene (PCE), the chemical most commonly used in dry cleaning is a health hazard. It pollutes water, may damage the ozone layer, and may cause cancer. When you bring your dry cleaning home, remove the plastic bags, and hang the clothes outside to air for several hours.

Technology is a double-edged sword. We appreciate all the conveniences it offers, but we must also be careful not to abuse it. Since televisions emit low-grade ionized radiation, sit ten feet away from the set while you're watching. Make sure your bed isn't near activated electrical plugs, and don't use an electric blanket. Avoid cooking food in a microwave oven. Get a shield for your computer screen. These shields are available at computer stores. If you use a laptop computer, don't sit with it on your lap for long periods of time. Put it on a table. And if you work all day long in a space that has fluorescent lighting, you might consider changing the lighting to a full spectrum light. Many health food stores carry these lights, which fit into a standard light fixture but are not as hard on the body.

## Arena IV

If some part of your body is out of alignment, then it must be brought back into alignment or it will upset the body chemistry. The reason a body goes out of alignment is because of a problem with tissue integrity. The tissues hold the bones in place. Because our tissues need protein to keep them strong, we have good tissue integrity if we are able to digest and metabolize the protein in our diet. When we are not getting the proper amount of protein—if the protein is not being digested well and is not being absorbed properly so that it can get into the cells to function—the tissue is compromised. The bones no longer stay in place.

There are a number of reasons why protein does not get to the cellular level to function. If you have been eating lots of sugar and have an elevated blood glucose level, your body has more difficulty digesting protein. It could be that you are not eating enough protein. Or you might be eating too much protein. The body is unable to process all of it, and it can back up in the system, causing problems. This will exhaust your enzymes for digesting protein, and the protein will become toxic to the body. If you are over-cooking foods containing protein, your body will not be able to digest it as well. Finally, you may need to look back at Arena I. You might be under distress when you eat your protein.

A chiropractor can correct your body's alignment problems. But if there is no tissue integrity, you will fall out of alignment again. It seems like a vicious circle, but you can stop it. Once you decide to commit yourself to a healthy lifestyle and stop upsetting your body, the body will heal itself. The tissue will regain integrity. When the chiropractor puts you into alignment, you will stay in alignment.

All four of these arenas are equally important in balancing the body, in maintaining homeostasis. Problems come from lifestyles that do not serve us well. There are some other unhappy aspects of this unbalance, but the simple outline above is enough for starters. I cannot stress enough that the repeated loss of homeostasis becomes a very serious problem. It can be the cause of "not feeling quite right" on a fairly regular basis and can lead to increasingly frequent problems with food and infections, and, indeed, to degenerative diseases of all kinds.

Now the question arises, "Without expensive tests, how can I find out what is upsetting my body chemistry?" The answer lies in determining the calcium-phosphorus balance, which is an indicator of the chemical balance throughout the body.

## Testing for Homeostasis

It is possible for you to discover those arenas that are giving you trouble, which foods are most likely to create imbalance in your body chemistry, and how well you are maintaining your health. Through use of the Body Chemistry Kit, you can discover if the foods you eat are being digested and metabolized properly. If you are experiencing stress, this kit will help you determine if that stress has become distress and is upsetting your body chemistry.

The test works by measuring the amount of calcium in the urine. It lets you know if you are secreting too much, too little, or a normal amount of calcium. Since calcium works only in relation to phosphorus, this test also indicates whether the phosphorus level is too high for the calcium present (no calcium will show up in the urine). If the phosphorus level is too low for the calcium present, too much calcium will show up in the urine.

Although the test detects only calcium, if the calcium-phosphorus ratio is out of balance, the rest of the minerals in the body are also out of balance. When the calcium-phosphorus ratio is properly balanced, the rest of the body's minerals are in balance. When minerals are in the right relationship, they function optimally, as do the vitamins and enzymes.

This home test kit for monitoring your body's chemical balance comes with a booklet that explains its use. See page 193 for ordering information.

## The Food Plans

The following food plans are effective in helping your body achieve homeostasis. If you experience symptoms such as headaches, allergies, joint pains, general fatigue (especially after meals), or high blood pressure, or if you have a degenerative disease, you might start out by following Food Plan I. If your symptoms are still present after a week, or if you are unable to maintain homeostasis (as determined by the Body Chemistry Test), try Food Plan II, which is more restrictive. Again, if symptoms still persist, go on to Food Plan III.

Keep in mind that by following the food plans, you may initiate withdrawal symptoms from the addictive foods, which are no longer in your diet. Omitting these foods can result in such painful symptoms as fever, depression, headaches, chills, anger, and fatigue. In some people, symptoms may last two or three days; for others, the symptoms may last a week.

## Food Plan I

Avoid all foods in categories IV and V (see food lists starting on page 147). Eat any other food.

If you are not beginning to feel better after being on Food Plan I for seven days, your body chemistry may require a more comprehensive food plan. Therefore, proceed with Food Plan II.

# Food Plan II

Avoid all foods in Categories III, IV, and V (see food lists starting on page 146). For meals, eat foods found in Category I. Foods in Category II may be eaten in small amounts and only between meals.

If you are still not experiencing better health after being on Food Plan II for seven days, you may need an even more restrictive plan. Proceed with Food Plan III.

# Food Plan III

It is clear that your unbalanced body chemistry involves more than just the foods common to body chemistry upset. Food Plan III is designed to provide complete nutrients to your body in their most bio-available form. Foods in this plan are the ones most people can digest, metabolize, and assimilate easily. The procedures and foods of Food Plan III are the least stressful to your body chemistry. Do the following:

For fourteen days, eat only those foods from Category I(see food lists starting on page 145). Eat one small portion from each food group four or five times a day.

If, after fourteen days, you are still not experiencing relief of symptoms and have addressed all four arenas, you will need to see a qualified practitioner who can test your blood for food sensitivities. You must find foods that do not upset your body chemistry.

# Food Categories

Choose foods from the following categories according to Food Plans I, II and III (pages 142-148.)

## Category I

When properly prepared and eaten, these are the foods that are best tolerated by those with an unbalanced body chemistry.

### GREEN LEAFY VEGETABLES

| | | |
|---|---|---|
| Artichoke | Cabbage | Lettuce (all) |
| Brussels sprouts | Kale | Spinach |

### GREEN VEGETABLES

| | | |
|---|---|---|
| Alfalfa | Broccoli | Okra |
| Asparagus | Celery | |
| Avocado* | Chinese pea pods | |

*Although avocado is a fruit, it is included in Category I foods.

### ROOT VEGETABLES

| | | |
|---|---|---|
| Jicama | Potato | Turnip |
| Onion | Radish | |
| Parsnip | Rutabaga | |

### YELLOW/WHITE VEGETABLES

| | |
|---|---|
| Cauliflower | Cucumber |
| Corn | Squash (all) |

### ORANGE/PURPLE/RED VEGETABLES

| | | |
|---|---|---|
| Beet | Eggplant | Sweet potato |
| Carrot | Pumpkin | Tomato |

### HERBS/CONDIMENTS

| | | |
|---|---|---|
| Arrowroot | Garlic | Rosehips |
| Basil | Ginger | Rosemary |
| Bay leaf | Horseradish | Safflower oil |
| Black pepper | Lemon | Sage |
| Butter | Lime | Sesame oil |
| Caraway | Mustard | Sunflower oil |
| Chili pepper | Nutmeg | Tarragon |
| Chive | Olive oil | Thyme |
| Cilantro | Oregano | |
| Dill | Parsley | |

## FISH

| | | |
|---|---|---|
| Anchovy | Halibut | Shark |
| Bass | Mackerel | Shrimp |
| Catfish | Oyster | Sole |
| Clam | Perch | Swordfish |
| Cod | Red snapper | Trout |
| Crab | Salmon | Tuna |
| Flounder | Sardine | Any other fish |
| Haddock | Scallop | |

## MEATS/POULTRY*

| | |
|---|---|
| Bacon | Liver (beef and chicken) |
| Beef | Pheasant |
| Chicken | Pork |
| Chicken eggs | Turkey |
| Duck | Venison |
| Lamb | |

## BEANS/GRAINS

| | | |
|---|---|---|
| Azuki beans | Kidney beans | Rice, brown |
| Barley | Lentils | (preferred) |
| Bean sprouts | Lima beans | Rice, white |
| Black beans | Millet | Rice, wild |
| Black-eyed peas | Navy beans | Rye |
| Buckwheat | Oats | Soybeans |
| Garbanzo beans | Pinto beans | Split peas |
| Green beans | Red beans | White beans |
| Green peas | | |

* Hopefully, you will be able to eat meat and poultry from free-range, organically fed animals.

If you are a vegetarian, eliminate foods from the Fish and the Meat/Poultry categories. Combine the beans and grains for complete protein.

## Category II

Some body chemistries are sensitive to these otherwise wholesome foods.

### FRUITS

| | | |
|---|---|---|
| Apples | Figs | Pears |
| Apricots | Grapes | Pineapples |
| Bananas | Guava | Raspberries |
| Cantaloupe | Melons (all) | Strawberries |
| Coconut | Nectarines | Watermelon |
| Cranberries | Papayas | |
| Dates | Peaches | |

### NUTS/SEEDS

| | | |
|---|---|---|
| Almonds | Hickory nuts | Poppy seeds |
| Brazil nuts | Macadamia nuts | Safflower seeds |
| Chestnuts | Pecans | Sunflower seeds |
| Hazelnuts | Pistachios | Walnuts |

### HERBS/CONDIMENTS

| | | |
|---|---|---|
| Anise seeds | Cream of tartar | Stevia |
| Chicory | Paprika | |
| Clove | Spearmint | |

## Category III

Overcooking, overeating, and eating foods with sugar have turned these normally well-tolerated foods into potentially abusive ones in some people. This includes those who have already compromised their systems through continued abuse.

### GRAINS

| | |
|---|---|
| Wheat bran | White flour |
| Wheat germ | Whole wheat |

## DAIRY
Buttermilk
Cheese (all)
Cream cheese
Milk, cow's
Whey
Yogurt
White flour
Whole wheat

## FUNGI
Mushrooms
Yeast, baker's
Yeast, brewer's

## FRUITS
Grapefruit
Mango
Orange
Tangerine

## NUTS/SEEDS
Cashews
Peanuts

## MISCELLANEOUS
Carob
Cinnamon
Coffee, regular
Coffee, decaf-
feinated
Cola bean
Corn gluten
Cornstarch
Curry
Hops
Molasses
Peppermint
Processed foods
Salt
Tea
Vanilla

**Category IV**

The following items are always abusive to human body chemistry. Only those who remain adaptive can rebalance after frequent exposure to the items listed here. The more Category IV foods consumed, the more rapid the deterioration in the body chemistry.

Alcohol
Barley malt
Beet sugar
Cane sugar
Cocoa
Corn sugar
Corn syrup
Fructose
Honey
Malt
Maple sugar
Rice syrup
Saccharin
Sucanot
Unrefined sugar

**Category V**

Items on the following list have been proven to unbalance the body chemistry. It serves your good health to stay away from these items or to use them sparingly and with caution. Some of these are used as preservatives, fillers, or coloring agents in processed foods. Be sure to read labels!

Acetaminophen
Aspirin
Baking powder
BHT (butylated
   hydroxytoluene)
Caffeine
Drugs: over-the-counter,
prescription, and street drugs

Food coloring
Formaldehyde
Ibuprofen
MSG
   (monosodium glutamate)
Petroleum by-products
Sodium benzoate
Tobacco

## Simple Suggestions for Breakfast and Snacks

People who are on Food Plan III and eat only Category I foods sometimes have difficulty with ideas for breakfast. Here are a few suggestions, many of which are also great as snacks.

- In the evening, cook some potatoes and refrigerate them. In the morning, slice them and sauté in butter.

- Baked potato with butter, guacamole, or pureed beans.

- Corn tortilla with butter, tomatoes, scrambled egg, and/or guacamole.

- Oatmeal with butter.

- Cream of Rice with butter.

- Rice cakes with sliced avocado, tomato, onion, green pepper, or cucumber.

- One-egg omelet with sliced tomato and diced vegetables (potato, green pepper, and onion are good choices).

- One-egg ranchero with corn tortilla.
- Cooked rice with butter.
- Steamed sweet potato with butter. Sweet potatoes are also good cold. They taste like candy.
- One cup of popped corn.
- Leftover rice heated with grated carrots, frozen peas, frozen lima beans, and butter. (This is my personal favorite.)

## Health-Promoting Eating Habits

Regardless of which food plan you are following, be sure to observe the following general health-promoting eating habits:

- Chew each mouthful of food at least twenty times.
- Do not wash foods down with liquids. Swallow your food before taking a drink.
- Consume portions you can easily digest.
- If you are emotionally upset or disturbed, eat smaller portions and chew your food longer than usual.
- Do not overcook your food.
- At each meal, consume as much raw food as you do cooked.
- Rather than eating large meals less often, consume smaller meals more often.
- Examine each meal and snack from the following viewpoint: "Will any part of this meal upset my body chemistry?"
- Eating small portions from a number of foods is far better than eating one large serving of a particular food.

Following these good eating habits will lessen the incidence of body chemistry imbalance and facilitate more efficient digestion, assimilation, and utilization of nutrients. In addition, you will be supporting your body's ability to rebalance its chemistry in spite of other lifestyle insults. Finally, your response to appropriate medical care will be enhanced.

We are all unique individuals. For some people, simple changes in diet and lifestyle can greatly improve their health. Others will need to explore many different modalities to help their bodies heal. Remember that what we put into our mouths, what comes out of our mouths, what we think, what we feel, what we do — every one of these affects our health. My observation is that what we put in our mouths is what is destroying us the fastest. We have to get back to basics. We must eat healthful food, drink pure water, breathe clean air, exercise, and keep a positive attitude. Although we live in a polluted society, it is our responsibility to remove the pollution from our bodies and to keep it out. Health or disease. The choice is yours.

# Glossary

**Abiogenesis**. A living force found in inorganic substances.

**Acid-base balance**. The balance between the amount of carbonic acid and bicarbonate in the blood. This must be maintained at a constant ratio of 1:20 in order to keep the hydrogen ion concentration of the plasma at a constant value. Any alteration in this ratio will disturb the acid-base balance of the blood and tissues and cause either acidosis or alkalosis. See **pH**.

**Adrenaline (epinephrine)**. One of the hormones secreted by the adrenal glands in response to physical or mental stress. Adrenaline initiates many bodily responses, including the stimulation of heart action and an increase in blood pressure, metabolic rate, and blood glucose concentration.

**Alimentary canal**. The food tract, which begins with the esophagus (food pipe) and extends for 20 to 25 feet to the rectum and anus. Also called the gastrointestinal tract.

**Allopathic**. A method of medical treatment in which the remedy (usually drugs) is directed at producing effects in the body that will directly oppose and alleviate the symptoms of disease.

**Alveolar bone**. The part of the upper and lower jawbone that supports the roots of the teeth.

**Analgesic**. Pain-relieving medication such as aspirin.

**Analogue**. A structure with a function similar to that of another structure.

**Anaerobic exercise**. A type of exercise that does not need extra oxygen but uses up the food stored in the muscles quickly, often within three to four minutes. Weight-lifting, wrestling, and sprinting are examples of anaerobic exercise.

**Anatomical**. Pertaining to anatomy, the study of the structure and organs of the body.

**Anthrax.** An infectious disease of farm animals which is caused by bacterium and can be transmitted to humans.

**Antigen (Allergen).** A foreign protein, as in a food, bacteria, or virus, that stimulates a specific immune response when introduced into the body.

**Antiseptic**. An agent which inhibits or destroys bacteria.

**Asepsis**. A sterile state wherein no germs are present.

**Asphyxia**. Suffocation

**Autonomic nervous system.** Made up of nerves, cells and fibers which cannot be controlled at will. Regulates involuntary actions, such as the intestines, heart and glands.

**Bacteria**. Usually one-celled organisms that are widely distributed in nature, live in the air, water, soil, animals, and plants. Many do not harm their hosts; others cause disease by producing poisons.

**Bicarbonate (HCO₃).** A salt of carbonic acid. It is present, as part of the alkali reserve, in the blood.

**Biological**. Pertaining to the study of plants and animals.

**Biophysics**. The physics of biological processes.

**Biotic**. The science of life and its activities.

**Body chemistry**. The functioning of the body systems which depend upon the body's chemical balance. It, in turn, depends upon balanced mineral relationships.

**Browning movement.** Also called the Maillard reaction, in which some foods discolor and toughen when they are cooked due to a chemical attachment of the sugar (glucose) in the food to protein. This reaction causes toast to turn brown and steak to toughen during cooking. It takes a high temperature to bind these glucose and protein molecules. This attachment changes the structure of the protein. Sometimes these particles are seen in the bloodstream.

**Buffer system.** The system that helps to preserve the balance of acidity or alkalinity of a solution.

**Candida Albicans.** An overgrowth of yeast-like fungus that normally grows within us. The overgrowth can affect the whole body adversely.

**Carbonic acid.** A chemical ($H_2Cl_3$) formed from carbon dioxide ($CO_2$) and water ($H_20$).

**Catalytic.** Hastening and stimulating a chemical reaction.

**Corpuscle.** Any cell in the body.

**Creosote.** A substance used in research to suppress the influence of atmospheric germs.

**Cretinism.** Severe thyroid deficiency or absent thyroid function occurring at birth or in infancy.

**Ecology.** The study of the relationships of humans, animals, and plants and the environment, including the way that human activities may affect other animal populations and alter natural surroundings.

**Electrolytes.** Substances which can, when in solution, convey an electrical impulse. Body electrolytes include sodium, potassium, chlorides, bicarbonate, and other elements.

**Embryological.** Growth and development of the fetus from fertilization of the ovum until birth.

**Endocrine system.** A network of ductless glands—the pituitary, thyroid, parathyroid, pancreas, and others — that secrete hormones into the bloodstream.

**Endogenous.** Something that originates from within the body. The opposite of exogenous.

**Environmental illness.** An illness causing people to react internally to anything in their environment.

**Enzyme.** A protein that acts as a biochemical catalyst to accelerate special chemical reactions, but does not itself undergo any change during the reaction. Digestive enzymes break down complex carbohydrates into simple sugars, fats or lipids into fatty acids, and glycerol, glycerides, and protein into amino acids.

**Epstein-Barr virus**. A virus causing infectious mononucleosis.

**Etiology**. The study of the cause of disease.

**Exocrine glands**. Glands which secrete onto the surface rather than into the blood (opposite of endocrine glands). The salivary glands are an example.

**Exogenous**. Arising from a source outside the body. (The opposite of endogenous.)

**Extracellular**. Outside the cells.

**Feedback System.** A system of signals sent to different parts of the body to help bring it back to balance when it has moved too far away from center.

**Fermentation**. The biochemical process by which organic substances, particularly carbohydrates, are decomposed and split into more simple compounds. Chemical energy for the process is provided by enzymes.

**Filament**. A fine, threadlike fiber. Filaments are found in most tissues and cells of the body and serve various functions. (Adj. filamentous.)

**Fluid matrix**. The intercellular substance of a tissue.

**Fructose**. A simple sugar found in fruit, corn syrup, honey, maple sugar, sucrose (table sugar) and other sweeteners. Although fructose metabolism is not dependent on insulin, it can have severe consequences on the white blood cells, the immune system.

**Fungus**. A simple plant that lacks chlorophyll. Fungi include yeast, molds, rust, and mushrooms. (Pl. fungi.)

**Galactose**. A simple sugar and a constituent of the milk sugar lactose. Galactose is converted to glucose in the liver.

**Gastroenterology**. The study of the gastrointestinal organs and their diseases, which also include diseases of the liver, biliary tract and pancreas.

**Germs**. Any microorganism, especially one that causes disease.

**Gingivitis**. Inflammation of the gums caused by plaque on the surfaces of the teeth at their necks. The gums are swollen and bleed easily.

**Globule**. Small round mass.

**Glucose**. A simple sugar, glucose is also called dextrose or grape sugar and is found in fruits, vegetables, tree sap, honey, corn syrup, molasses, and table sugar. It is an end product of the digestion of starch, sucrose, maltose, and lactose, and provides most of the energy for the cells of the body.

**Glycogen**. A major carbohydrate stored in the liver and muscles, glycogen is changed to glucose and released into the bloodstream as needed by the body for energy.

**Glyconeogenic pathway.** The biochemical process in which glucose is synthesized from fats and/or amino acids (proteins). This process occurs mainly in the liver and kidney and meets the needs of the body for glucose when carbohydrate is not available in sufficient amounts in the diet.

**Goiter**. An enlargement of the thyroid gland which causes swelling in the neck. It may involve the entire gland or only parts of it.

**Growth hormone (GH).** A hormone secreted by the post-pituitary in the base of the skull. GH promotes growth of the long bones in the limbs and increases protein synthesis.

**Hematological**. Having to do with the diseases of the blood and blood-forming organs.

**Hepatic**. Referring to the liver.

**Heterogenesis**. A living force found in organic material.

**Histological**. Pertaining to the science that deals with the minute structure of cells, tissues, and organs in their relation to their function.

**Homeostasis**. The state of equilibrium (balance between opposing pressures) in the body with respect to various functions and to the chemical compositions of the fluids and tissues—e.g., pH, temperature, heart rate, blood pressure, water content, blood sugar, etc.

**Homeostatic mechanism.** A mechanism used by the body to maintain a stable chemical internal environment, despite external change. This is accomplished in large part by the hormones.

**Hormone**. A substance secreted by a gland, a hormone travels throughout the bloodstream to a target organ or tissue, where it acts to modify the organ or tissue's structure or function.

**Hyperglycemic**. A condition characterized by excessive sugar in the blood.

**Hyperthermia**. A higher than normal body temperature.

**Hypoglycemic**. A condition characterized by too little sugar in the blood.

**Hypothalamus**. Literally below the thalamus in the lower brain. This is the highest center of the autonomic nervous system, controlling various physiological functions such as hunger, thirst, emotions, and the body's twenty-four-hour clock. Performs important endocrine functions, producing, releasing and inhibiting some hormones that act on the anterior pituitary and regulate the release of hormones.

**Hypothermia**. A lower than normal body temperature.

**Inert**. Inactive, devoid of active chemical properties.

**Infusion**. A solution produced by steeping extracted plant or animal matter in boiling water.

**Inorganic**. Not containing matter originating from plant or animal life.

**Intracellular**. Inside the cells.

**Kinesiology**. The scientific study of muscular activity and of anatomy, physiology, and the mechanics of body movement.

**Labile cells.** Cells that have the ability to be altered or change.

**Lactic**. Pertaining to milk.

**Latent**. Pertaining to a condition that is inactive or is existing as a potential problem.

**Lymphatic**. Vessel or channel that carries lymph.

**Metabolic rate.** The rate at which food is broken down in the body.

**Metabolism**. The process by which foods are transformed into basic elements that can be utilized by the body for energy or growth.

**Metamorphose.** To change in form, structure or function.

**Microorganism (microbe).** Any organism too small to be visible to the naked eye. Microorganisms, may or may not cause disease and include bacteria, viruses, some fungi, mycoplasmas, protozoan and rickettsias.

**Microzyma.** Organized and living ferments.

**Milieu intérieur.** The internal environment, the fluids bathing the tissue cells of multicellular animals.

**Molecular granular.** Small ferment. Also known as microzyma.

**Molecule.** The smallest particle of a substance that exhibits all its properties.

**Monomorphism.** Of one shape, unchanging in shape.

**Monosaccharide.** A simple sugar having the general formula $(CH_2O)$.

**Morphological.** The differences in forms between species.

**Mycelium.** The tangled mass of fine, branching threads that make up the feeding and growing part of a fungus.

**Neurotransmitter.** Any chemical that changes or results in the sending of nerve signals across spaces, such as acetylcholine, epinephrine, and norepinephrine.

**Organic.** Describing chemical compounds containing carbon, found in all living systems.

**Organism.** Any living animal or plant which may consist of a single cell or a group of differentiated but interdependent cells.

**Paradigm.** An example that serves as a pattern or model.

**Parasympathetic nervous system.** Part of the autonomic nervous system. Its actions begin by the release of a chemical (acetylcholine) and affect body resources. Parasympathetic nerve fibers slow the heart and cause intestine activity (peristalsis). They also help release fluids from tear, saliva, and digestion glands. They begin the release of bile and insulin, widen some blood vessels, and narrow the pupils, esophagus, and tubes of the lung. They also relax muscles during urination and defecation.

**Pasteurization.** The heating of milk products, wine, fruits juices, etc., for about thirty minutes at 154.4%F (80%C).

**Pathogen.** A bacteria or virus capable of causing disease.

**Pathological.** Related to or pertaining to disease on the basis of an examination of the diseased tissue.

**Periodontal disease.** A disease of the tissues surrounding the teeth.

**Peristalsis/Peristaltic.** Contractions of the intestines, occurring in waves, which propel the intestinal contents (food) onward. This occurs involuntarily.

**Pertussis.** Whooping cough.

**pH.** A scale denoting the acidity or alkalinity of a solution. A solution of pH 7 is neutral, below 7 is acidic, above 7 is alkaline.

**Phagocyte.** Part of the immune system, a cell that can destroy either foreign matter or bacteria.

**Phenolic acid.** A substance used to suppress the influence of atmospheric germs in experiments.

**Physicochemical.** Relating to both physics and chemistry, such as to the field of physical chemistry.

**Physiology.** The science dealing with the study of the function of tissues or organs.

**Plasma.** The straw-colored fluid portion of the blood in which the red and white cells are suspended.

**Pleomorphism.** Condition in which a living organism assumes a number of forms during its life cycle.

**Polysaccharide.** A carbohydrate, such as a starch, formed from many monosaccharides joined together in long, branched chains.

**Protozoa.** One-celled animals, the lowest form of life. Disease causing parasites in man.

**Psychosomatic.** Related to or involving both the body and the mind, usually applied to illnesses that are caused by the interaction of mental and physical factors.

**Putrefaction**. Decomposition of tissues.

**Reflexology**. A system of treating some disorders by massaging the soles of the feet, using methods like those of acupuncture.

**Rolfing**. A method of deep massage intended to realign the body by changing the length and tone of certain tissues.

**Secondary polycythemia.** An increase in the hemoglobin concentration of the blood.

**Serology**. The branch of clinical medicine that studies the serum of the blood.

**Serum**. Part of whole blood that remains after blood has clotted. It is yellowish in color.

**Somatic**. Relating to the body, physical.

**Spontaneous generation.** The principle that states living organisms can arise, independent of any parent, from inorganic matter (abiogenesis) or organic debris (heterogenesis).

**Spore**. A form taken by some bacteria that is resistant to heat, drying, or chemicals. Under proper conditions, a spore may turn back into the active form of the bacterium.

**Stabile cells.** Fixed, steady cells. The opposite of labile. Unaffected by ordinary degrees of heat.

**Subcortical**. Part of the brain below the cortex.

**Sympathetic nervous system.** Part of the autonomic nervous system that speeds up heart rate, narrows blood vessels, and raises heart rate.

**Terrain**. Biological terrain, interior environment, the body chemistry.

**Vesicle**. Any small bladder, especially one filled with fluid.

**Vibrio**. Any bacterium that is able to move.

**Virulent**. The ability of a microorganism to cause disease.

**Virus**. Smaller than a bacteria, can only grow in living cells, and is capable of causing infectious diseases.

# Notes

## Chapter 1

1. *1994 – US. Department of Health and Human Services.* (Hyattsville, MD: National Center for Health Statistics, 1994.)

2. *Morbidity and Mortality Weekly Report,* 46 (October 30, 1997), pp. 1013-1026.

3. *World Health Statistics* (Geneva, Switzerland: World Health Organization, 1994)

4. Robert W Pinner et al. "Trends in Infectious Diseases Mortality in the United States." *Journal of the American Medical Association* 275, no. 3 (1996), pp. 189-193.

5. Shapiro, Andrew L. *We're Number One! Where America Stands and Falls in the New World Order.* (New York: Vintage, 1992.)

## Chapter 2

1. Emanuel Cheraskin. "Human Health and Homeostasis," II. *International Journal of Biosocial and Medical Research* 13, no. 1 (1991), p. 30.

2. Ibid, pp. 31-32.

3. E Cheraskin, W.M. Ringsdorf Jr., A.T.S.H. Setyaadmadja, et al. "The Birmingham, Alabama 1964 Diabetes Detection Drive: III Sex and Dextrostix Patterns." *Alabama Journal of Medical Science*, no. 4 (1967), pp. 239-291.

4. Nancy Appleton. *Lick the Sugar Habit.* (Garden City Park, NY: Avery Publishing Group, 1996.)

5. R D. Williams. "Nature, Nurture and Family Predisposition." *New England Journal of Medicine* 318 (1988), pp. 769l-7692.

6. René Dubos. *Man Adapting.* (New Haven, CT: Yale University Press, 1965.)

7. F. Adams. *The Genuine Works of Hippocrates.* (Baltimore, MD: Williams and Wilkins Company, 1939.)

8. *Encyclopedia Americana,* 1997 ed, s.v. "Medicine, history."

9. C. West Churchman. *The Systems Approach and its Enemies.* (New York: Basic Books, Inc., 1979.) p. 39.

10. Galen (Claudius Galenus). *Galen, on the Natural Faculties.* Translated by John Brock. (New York: G. P. Putnam and Sons, 1916.)

11. *Encyclopedia Americana*, sv. "Medicine, history."

12. Ibid, sv. "Middle Ages, medicine."

13. C Alberto Seguin. "The Concept of Disease." *Psychosomatic Medicine* 8 (1946), pp. 252-253.

## Chapter 3

1. Jacques Nicolle. *Louis Pasteur –The Story of His Major Discoveries.* (Philadelphia: Basic Books, Inc., 1920.) p. 148.

2. Imago Galdston. "Beyond the Germ Theory: The Roles of Deprivation and Stress in Health and Disease." *Beyond the Germ Theory*, edited by Imago Galdston. (New York: New York Academy of Medicine Book, 1951.) p. 6.

3. Ibid.

4. Wilhelm Reich. *The Cancer Biopathy*, (New York: Farrar, Straus and Giroux, 1973.) p. viii.

5. René Dubos. "Pasteur and Modern Science." *Pasteur Fermentation Centennial, 1847-1957.* (New York: Charles Pfizer & Co., Inc., 1958.) pp. 17-32.

6. Ibid.

7. Ibid.

8. Louis Pasteur. "The Physiological Theory of Fermentation." 1879. Translated by F. Faulkner and D.C. Robb. *Harvard Classics* 38. (New York: P.F. Collier & Son, 1938.) pp. 275-363.

9. Émile Duclaux. *Pasteur – The History of a Mind*, translated by Erwin F. Smith and Florence Hedges. (Philadelphia: W.B. Saunders Company, 1920.) pp. 193-97.

10. René Dubos. *Louis Pasteur: Free Lance of Science*, 2nd rev. ed. (New York: Charles Scribner's Sons, 1976.) p. 168.

11. Louis Pasteur. "The Germ Theory and its Applications to Medicine and Surgery." Paper read before the French Academy of Sciences, April 29, 1878. Translated by H.C. Ernst. *Harvard Classics* 38. (New York: P.F. Collier & Son, 1938.) p. 364.

12. Louis Pasteur. "Louis Pasteur's Credo of Science: His Address When He Was Inducted into the French Academy," translated by Eli Moschocwitz. *Bulletin of the History of Medicine* 22 (1989), pp. 528-48.

13. JR. Verner et al. *Rational Bacteriology*, 2nd ed. (New York: H. Wolff, 1953.) p. 158.

14. Dubos, "Pasteur and Modern Science," pp. 17-32.

15. Pasteur, "Louis Pasteur's Credo of Science: His Address When He Was Inducted into the French Academy," pp. 528-48.

16. Félix Archimède Pouchet. *Heterogenesis: A Treatise on Spontaneous Generation.* 1859.

17. Ibid.

18. John Farley. *The Spontaneous Generation Controversy from Descartes to Oparin.* (Baltimore, MD: Johns Hopkins University Press, 1977.) p. 1.

19. John Farley and Gerald Geison. "Science, Politics and Spontaneous Generation in Nineteenth-Century France: The Pasteur–Pouchet Debate," *Bulletin of the History of Medicine* 48, no. 2 (1994), p. 170.

20. Ibid.

21. Farley, p. 106.

22. Farley, p. 110.

23. Farley, p. 111.

24. Ibid.

25. Paul de Kruif. *Microbe Hunters.* (New York: Harcourt, Brace and World, Inc., 1953.)

26. K Codell Carter. "The Development of Pasteur's Concept of Disease Causation and the Emergence of Specific Causes in Nineteenth-Century Medicine." *Bulletin of the History of Medicine* 65 (1989), pp. 528-48.

27. Louis Pasteur. *Pasteur's and Tyndall's Study of Spontaneous Generation, Harvard Case Histories in Experimental Science, Case 7,* edited by James Bryant Conant. (Cambridge, MA: Harvard University Press, 1953.) p. 60.

28. Louis Pasteur. *Œuvres de Pasteur* II, seven volumes edited by Louis Pasteur and Pasteur Vallery-Radot. (Paris: Masson, 1861.)

29. Ibid, p. 191.

30. Ibid.

31. Farley and Geison, p. 171.

32. René Dubos. *Louis Pasteur – Free Lance of Science,* 1st ed. (New York: Charles Scribner's Sons, 1960); *Louis Pasteur – Free Lance of Science,* 2nd rev. ed. (New York: Charles Scribner's Sons, 1976.); "Pasteur and Modern Science," *Pasteur Fermentation Centennial,* 1847–1957. (New York: Charles Pfizer & Co. Inc., 1958.); *Pasteur and Modern Science,* 1st ed. (New York: Doubleday and Co., 1960.); *Pasteur and Modern Science,* 2nd ed. (New York: Doubleday and Co., 1988.)

33. Dubos, 1976, xvii-xxxix.

34. Ibid.

35. Ibid.

36. Hilaire Cuny. *Louis Pasteur – The Man and His Theories*, translated by Patrick Evans. (London: Souvenir Press, 1948.); Jacques Nicolle. *Louis Pasteur – The Story of His Major Discoveries.* (Philadelphia: Basic Books, Inc., 1920.); Stephen Paget. *Pasteur and After Pasteur.* (London: Adam and Charles Black, 1917.); *The World of René Dubos – A Collection from His Writings*, edited by Gerald Piel and Osborn Segerberg, Jr. (New York: Henry Holt and Company, 1990.); René Vallery-Radot. *Louis Pasteur – A Great Life in Brief,* translated by Alfred Joseph. (New York: Alfred A. Knopf, 1960.); René Vallery-Radot. *The Life of Pasteur,* translated by Mrs. R.L. Devonshire. (New York: Doubleday, Doran, 1938.)

37. Duclaux, p. 109-111.

38. Ibid.

39. Christine Russell. "Louis Pasteur and Questions of Fraud," *Townsend Letter for Doctors* (October 1993), p. 960.

40. Ibid.

41. Ibid.

42. Geison, pp. 172-176.

43. Ibid.

44. Ibid.

45. Ibid, pp. 250-252.

46. Ibid.

47. Ibid.

48. Russell, p. 960.

## Chapter 4

1. Imago Galdston. "Beyond the Germ Theory: The Roles of Deprivation and Stress in Health and Disease." *Beyond the Germ Theory*, edited by Imago Galdston. (New York: New York Academy of Medicine Book, 1951.) p. 14.

2. Claude Bernard. "Lessons on the Phenomena of Life Common to Animals and Vegetables." (1878) *Homeostasis: Origin of the Concept*, edited by L.L. Langley. (Stroudburg, PA: Dowden, Hutchinson, Ross and Co, 1973.) pp. 23-48.

3. Richard H. Hardy. *Homeostasis, Studies in Biology* 63. (London: Edward Arnold Limited, 1982.) p. 1.

4. Galdston, p. 8.

5. Ibid.

6. J.M.D. Olmsted and I. Harris Olmsted. *Claude Bernard and the Experimental Method in Medicine.* (New York: Henry Schuman, 1952.) p. 107.

7. Andrew Robert Aisenberg. "Contagious Disease and the Government of Paris in the Age of Pasteur." Ph.D. dissertation, Yale University, 1993, p. 54-55.

8. Ibid.

9. Claude Bernard. "Experimental Considerations Common to Living Things and Inorganic Bodies." *Homeostasis: Origin of the Concept*, edited by L.L. Langley. (Stroudburg, PA: Dowden, Hutchinson, Ross and Co., 1973.) pp. 133-135.

10. Frederic L Holmes. "Origins of the Concept of the Milieu Intérieur." *Claude Bernard and Experimental Medicine*, edited by Francisco Grande and Maurice B. Visscher. (Cambridge, MS: Schenkman Publishing Company, Inc., 1967), pp. 189-190.

11. Ibid.

12. Claude Bernard. *An Introduction to the Study of Experimental Medicine* (1865). Translated by H.C. Greene. (New York: Dover, 1957.) pp. 104.

13. Bernard, 1865, p. 104.

14. John Farley. *The Spontaneous Generation Controversy from Descartes to Oparin.* (Baltimore, MD: Johns Hopkins University Press, 1977.) p. 113.

15. Frederic L Holmes. "Claude Bernard, The Milieu Intérieur, and Regulatory Physiology." *History of Physiology* 8 (1986), pp. 3-25.

16. *Encyclopedia Britannica.* 1959 edition, s.v "Bernard, Claude."

17. Marie Nonclercq. *Antoine Béchamp, 1816- 1908: L'homme et le savant, originalité et fécondité de son œuvre.* [Antoine Béchamp, 1816-1908: the man and the scientist, the originality and the fertility of his research] (Paris: Maloine, 1982.)

18. Florence Nightingale. *Notes on Nursing* (1859). Reprint. (Philadelphia: J. B. Lippincott Company, 1946.) p. 19.

## Chapter 5

1. Béchamp, *Les Microzymas,* p. 38.

2. Gerald L Geison. *The Private Science of Louis Pasteur.* (Princeton, NJ: Princeton University Press, 1995.) p. 275.

3. Christopher Bird. *The Persecution and Trial of Gaston Naessens.* (Tiburon, CA: H.J. Kramer Inc., 1991.) p. 7.

4. Alan Cantwell, Jr. *Cancer Microbe.* (Los Angeles: Aries Rising Press, 1990.) p. 131.

5. Béchamp to Senator JB. Dumas, Dossier Dumas, Library of the Academy of Science, Paris.

6. Antoine Béchamp. *The Blood and its Third Anatomical Element,* translated by Montague R. Leverson. (London: John Ousley Limited, 1912.) vii.

7. Ibid, p. 5.

8. Harris Coulter. *Divided Legacy: A History of the Schism in Medical Thought,* Vol.IV. (Washington, DC: Wehawken Book Co., 1995.) p. 30.

9. E Douglas Hume. *Béchamp or Pasteur? A Lost Chapter in the History of Biology.* (Ashingdon, Rochford, Essex, England: C.W. Daniel Company Limited, 1947.) pp. 123-124.

10. Béchamp to Dumas, 1882

11. Antoine Béchamp. "Nutrition." Presentation to the Conference at Lyon, France, for the Montpellier Medical Society, August, 1868. Library of the Academy of Science, Paris.

12. Hume, p. 80.

13. R.B. Pearson. *The Dream and Lie of Louis Pasteur.* (Collingswood, Victoria, Australia: Sumeria, no date.) p. 19.

14. Ibid.

15. Hume, p. 80.

16. Ibid.

17. Béchamp, *The Blood and Its Third Anatomical Element*, p. 17.

18. Béchamp to Dumas, September 26, 1865

19. A Kalokerinos and G.C. Dettman. "Second Thoughts about Disease – A Controversy and Béchamp Revisited." *Journal of the International Academy of Preventive Medicine* IV, no. 1 (July, 1977), pp. 4-24.

20. Pearson, p. 18.

21. Béchamp, *The Blood and Its Third Anatomical Element*, p. 240.

22. Ernst Almquist. "Variation and Life Cycle of Pathogenic Bacteria" Journal of Infectious Diseases 33 (1922), pp. 483-493.

23. Louis Pasteur. "The Germ Theory and Its Applications to Medicine and Surgery." Paper read before the French Academy of Sciences, April 29, 1878. Translated by H.C. Ernst. *Harvard Classics* 38. (New York: F.P. Collier & Sons, 1938.) p. 364.

24. Hume, p. 209.

25. Ibid, p. 210.

26. Geison, p. 19.

27. Pearson, p. 18.

28. Pasteur, "The Germ Theory and Its Applications to Medicine and Surgery," p. 368.

29. John Farley. The Spontaneous Generation Controversy from Descartes to Oparin. (Baltimore, MD: Johns Hopkins University Press, 1977.) p. 101.

30. Béchamp to the Academy of Medicine, May 3, 1870 Dossier letters. Library of the Academy of Science, Paris.

31. Béchamp, *The Blood and Its Third Anatomical Element*, pp. 197-198.

32. Ibid, p. 45.

33. Ibid, p. 21.

34. Pearson, p. 18.

35. Ibid, p. 20.

36. Lida H Mattman. *Cell Wall Deficient Forms.* (Ann Arbor, MI: CRC Press, 1992.) p. 241.

37. Marie Nonclercq. *Antoine Béchamp, 1816-1908: L'homme et le savant, originalité et fecondité de son œuvre.* [Antoine Béchamp, 1816-1908: the man and the scientist, the originality and the fertility of his research] (Paris: Maloine, 1982.) pp. 198-199.

38. Verner et al, p. 297.

39. *Health Freedom News* (July/August 1992), pp. 15-18.

40. Cantwell, p. 151.

## Chapter 6

1. Walter B Cannon. *The Wisdom of the Body*, 2nd edition. (New York: Norton, 1939.) xv.

2. Saul Benison, Clifford Barger and Elin L Wolfe. *Walter B. Cannon – The Life and Times of a Young Scientist.* (Cambridge, MS: Belknap Press of Harvard University, 1987.)

3. Walter B Cannon. *The Mechanical Factors of Digestion.* (London: Edward Arnold, 1891.)

4. Walter B Cannon. "The Movements of the Stomach Studied by Means of the Roentgen Rays." *American Journal of Physiology 1* (1898), pp. 359-382.

5. Walter B Cannon. "The Movements of the Intestines Studied by Means of the Roentgen Rays." *American Journal of Physiology 6* (1902), pp. 251-277 and xxvii.

6. Cannon, *The Mechanical Factors of Digestion*

7. Charles Darwin. *Expression of the Emotions in Man and Animals.* (London: John Murray, 1872.)

8. Carl George Lange and William James. *The Emotions.* (New York: Hafner Publishing, 1967.)

9. Ivan P Pavlov. *Lectures on Conditioned Reflexes: Twenty-five Years of Objective Study of the Higher Nervous Activity of Animals*, translated by W. Horsley Gantt. (New York: International Publishers Co., 1928.)

10. Donald Fleming. "Walter B. Cannon and Homeostasis." *Social Research* 51, no. 3 (Autumn 1984), p. 629.

11. William Douglass. *Introduction to Social Psychology.* 1908.

12. Walter B Cannon. "The Utility of Bodily Changes in Fear, Rage and Pain." *Harvard Graduates Magazine* 22 (1913-1914), pp. 570-573.

13. Walter B Cannon. *Bodily Changes in Pain, Hunger, Fear and Rage.* (New York: D. Appleton and Co., 1915.)

14. Walter B Cannon. *Traumatic Shock.* (New York: D. Appleton and Co., 1923.)

15. Fleming, p. 613.

16 Fleming, p. 629.

17. Walter B Cannon. *Bodily Changes in Pain, Hunger, Fear and Rage* 2nd edition. (New York: D. Appleton and Company, 1929.)

18. Walter B Cannon. "The Influence of Emotional States on the Functions of the Alimentary Canal." *American Journal of Medical Sciences* (April 1909), pp. 64-69.

19. Charles Richet. *Dictionnaire de Physiologie* Vol. IV. Paris: F. Alcan, 1895.

20. Cannon, *The Wisdom of the Body* 2nd ed., p. 28.

21. Ibid, p. 232.

22. Benison et al, p. 53.

## Chapter 7

1. Bob Jackson. "Melvin E. Page, D.D.S. – The Story of a Nutritional Pioneer – 1894-1983." *Price-Pottenger Nutrition Foundation Health Journal* 19, no. 4 (Winter 1995), pp. 7-9.

2. Melvin E. Page and Leon H. Abrams Jr. *Health Versus Disease* (St. Petersburg Beach, FL: The Page Foundation Inc., 1960.)

3. Walter B. Cannon. "Organization for Physiological Homeostasis." *Physiological Review* 9 (1929), p. 426.

4. Jackson, pp. 7-9.

5. Melvin E. Page. *Body Chemistry in Health and Disease.* (St. Petersburg Beach, FL: Nutritional Development, c. 1963.) p. 14.

6. Melvin E. Page and Leon Adams Jr. *Your Body Is Your Best Doctor.* (New Canaan, CT: Keats Publishing, 1972.) p. 17.

7. Jackson, pp. 7-9.

8. Melvin E. Page. *Degeneration – Regeneration.* (San Diego, CA: Price-Pottenger Nutritional Foundation, 1949.) p. 12.

9. Ibid, p. 13.

10. I am grateful for the knowledge that Pacetti has given me about body chemistry. I have used this method in my counseling and in my research. Many people have had medical symptoms disappear when they have removed foods that are not metabolizing correctly, exercise, and not let stress become distress. It is so simple and for many so hard to do.

11. Ibid, p. 19.

12. Page, *Body Chemistry in Health and Disease*, p. 9.

13. Page, *Degeneration – Regeneration*, p. 14.

14. Page, *Your Body is Your Best Doctor*, p. 26.

15. Weston A. Price. *Nutrition and Physical Degeneration*. (La Mesa, CA: Price Pottenger Nutritional Foundation, 1945, reprint 1970.)

16. Page, *Degeneration – Regeneration*, p. 93.

17. Price, p. 4.

18. Jackson, pp. 7-9.

19. Page, *Degeneration – Regeneration*, p. 14.

## Chapter 8

1. Erik Enby et al. *Hidden Killers: The Revolutionary Medical Discoveries of Professor Guenther Enderlein*. (Sheehane Communications, 1990.) pp. 2-6.

2. Guenther Enderlien. *Bakterien Cyclogenie* [The life cycle of bacteria] (Berlin: De Gruyter, 1925.)

3. Harris Coulter. *Divided Legacy –A History of the Schism in Medical Thought* IV. (Washington, DC: Center for Empirical Medicine, 1994.) pp. 189-191.

4. *Health Freedom News* (July/August 1992), pp. 15-18.

5. Enby et al, p. 25.

6. Christopher Bird. "The Mystery of Pleomorphic (Form-Changing) Microbial Organisms: One Brief Overview." Paper presented at the Symposium 1991: From Béchamp's Microzyma to the Somatid Theory: Somatidian Orthobiology, Sherbrooke, Quebec, Canada at Centre d'Orthobiologie Somatidienne Inc. (June 8-9, 1991), p. 16.

7. Enby et al, p. 24.

8. Ibid, p. 33.

9. Ibid, p. 4.

10. Ibid, p. 34.

11. Ibid, p. 1.

12. Enderlein, p. 41.

13. Coulter, p. 192.

14. Christopher Bird. *The Persecution and Trial of Gaston Naessens*. (Tiburon, CA: H.J. Kramer Inc., 1991.) p. 272.

15. Alison Davidson, compiled. *The Royal R Rife Report*. (Bayside, CA: Borderland Sciences, no date.) p. 58.

16. Edward C Rosenow. "Transmutations within the Streptococcus-Pneumococcus Group." *Journal of Infectious Diseases* 14, no. 1, (January 1914), pp. 1-32.

17. Royal Raymond Rife and Arthur Isaac Kendall. "Observations on Bacillus Typhosus in its Filterable State." *California and Western Medicine* xxxv, no. 6 (December 1931), pp. 109-111.

18. Christopher Bird. "What Has Become of the Rife Microscope?" *New Age* (March, 1976), pp. 41-47.

19. Ibid.

20. Ibid.

21. Ibid.

22. "Rife's Microscope," *The Smithsonian Report*, Annual Report of the Board of Regents of the Smithsonian Institution, 1944.

23. Ibid.

24. Bird, *The Persecution and Trial of Gaston Naessens*, pp. 275-291.

25. "Filterable Bodies Seen with the Rife Microscope" *Science-Supplement, Science* (December 11, 1931.)

26. "Is a New Field About to Be Opened in the Science of Bacteriology?" ed, *California and Western Medicine* 36, no. 6 (December, 1931), p. 461.

27. Bird, *The Persecution and Trial of Gaston Naessens*, p. 291.

28. Ibid.

29. Alan Cantwell, Jr. *Cancer Microbe*. (Los Angeles: Aries Rising Press, 1990.) pp. 155-183.

30. Ibid

31. Myron Sharaf. *Fury on Earth – A Biography of Wilhelm Reich*. (New York: St. Martin's Press/Marek, 1983.) pp. 222-223.

32. Ibid.

33. Ibid.

34. Bird, *The Persecution and Trial of Gaston Naessens*, p. 270.

35. Ibid.

36. Ibid.

37. Ibid, p. 290.

38. Wilhelm Reich. *The Bion Experiments*. (New York: Farrar, Straus & Giroux, 1979.) p. 28.

39. Christopher Bird. "To Be or Not To Be." *The American Raum & Zeit* 2, no. 6 (1991), pp. 52-59.

40. Coulter, pp. 349-350.

## Chapter 9

1. Christopher Bird. *The Persecution and Trial of Gaston Naessens.* (Tiburon, CA: H.J. Kramer Inc., 1991.) p. 19.

2. Leslie Kenton. "What the Microscope Can Reveal." *International Journal of Alternative and Complementary Medicine* 10, no. 1 (January, 1992), pp. 11-12.

3. Bird. *The Persecution and Trial of Gaston Naessens* pp. 300-301.

4. Christopher Bird. "Somatids, 714-X and Curing Cancer – Gaston Naessens and the New Biology: Part II" *Bio/Tech News* (1993-94 Special Issue), p. 6.

5. Kenton, pp. 11-12.

6. Bird, *The Persecution and Trial of Gaston Naessens*, xiii-xiv

7. Christopher Bird. "The Tragedy of Innovation and Inventors Working on the Frontiers of Science." *The American Raum & Zeit* 2, no. 3, 1991, p. 40.

8. Ibid.

9. Ibid, p. 21.

10. Bird, *The Persecution and Trial of Gaston Naessens*, pp. 2-16.

11. Sterling Edwards and Peter Edwards. *Alex Carrel – Visionary Surgeon.* (Springfield, IL: Thomas Pub., 1939.)

12. Bird, "Somatids, 714-X and Curing Cancer . ."

13. Ibid.

14. Ibid.

15. Christopher Bird. "Seeing is Believing – Gaston Naessens and the New Biology: Part I." *Bio/Tech News.* (1993-94 Special Issue), p. 5.

16. Gaston Naessens. Centre Expérimentale de Recherches Biologiques de l'Estrie Inc, 5260 Rue Mills, Rock Forest, Quebec, J1N 3B6, Canada.

17. http://www.livelinks.com/sumeria/tech/naessens.html

## Chapter 10

1. Harold E Buttram. "Overuse of Antibiotics and the Need for Alternatives." *Townsend Letter for Doctors* (November 1991), pp. 867-869.

2. *Time Magazine* (April 27, 1998) "Medicine."

3. Dennis Kelly. "Many Elderly Given Inappropriate Drugs." *USA Today* (August 8, 1995), 1A. These disorders include autism, speech and language problems, multi-system developmental disorders, skin irritations, sleep disturbances, repetitive behavior, and loss of language.

4. "Colloidal Silver Offers Possible Solution to Antibiotics Crisis" *Well Mind Association of Greater Washington* 219 (October 1995), pp. 4-5.

5. William Crook. *The Yeast Connection*. (Jackson, TN: Professional Books, 1983.) p. 16.

6. Imago Galdston. *The Meaning of Social Medicine*. (Cambridge, MS: Harvard University Press, 1954.) pp. 81-83.

7. Patricia Lemer and Kelly Dorfman. "Survey Shows Link Between Antibiotics and Developmental Delays in Children." *Townsend Newsletter for Doctors* (October 1995), p. 9.

8. Sidney M Wolfe. "Adverse Drug Reactions: Why Do They Occur and How Serious Is the Problem?" *Health Letter* 10 (October 1993), pp. 1-3, 6.

9. Loren Hunt and Edward Rosenow "Asthma-Producing Drugs." *Annals of Allergy* 68 (June 1992), pp. 453-462.

10. "Drugs That Cause Psychiatric Symptoms" *Medical Letter* 31, no. 808 (December 29, 1989), p. 31.

11. "Formula Determines Risk for NSAID-Associated Gastropathy" *Geriatrics* 45, no. 9 (September 9, 1990), p. 25.

12. Ty Cobb "Your Health Philosophy: The Most Important Part of Your Practice." *Townsend Letter for Doctors* (April 1995) p. 101-102.

13. KR. Stratton, C.J. Howe and R.B. Johnston Jr. "Adverse Events Associated with Childhood Vaccines: Evidence Bearing on Causality." *Journal of the American Medical Association* 271, no. 20 (May 25, 1994), pp. 1602-1605.

14. P. Duclos and A. Bentsi-Enchil. "Current Thoughts on the Risks and Benefits of Immunization." *Drug Safety* 8, no. 6 (1993), pp. 404-413.

15. J.R. Verner, C.W. Weiant, and R.J. Watkins. *Rational Bacteriology*. (New York: H. Wolff, 1953.) p. 175.

16. Ibid, p. 179.

17. Neil Z. Miller. *Vaccines: Are They Really Safe and Effective?* (Santa Fe, NM: New Atlantean Press, 1994.) pp. 17-40.

18. Celia Christie, Mary L Marx, Colin D. Marchant, and Shirley F. Reising. "The 1993 Epidemic of Pertussis in Cincinnati: Resurgence of Disease in a Highly Immunized Population of Children." *New England Journal of Medicine* 331, no. 1 (July 7, 1994), pp. 16-21.

19. Mark Bello. "A Look at the Prognosis and Economics of Heart Disease." *News Report* (December 1990-January 1991), pp. 13-15.

20. Commerce Department of the US. Federal Government. *U.S. Industrial Outlook*. 1994, pp. 74-75.

21. Tristam Coffin, ed. "The Health Care Crisis." *The Washington Spectator* 14 no. 14 (August 1, 1991), pp. 1-4.

22. US. Bureau of Census, *Statistical Abstract of the United States* 114th edition. (Washington DC, 1994.) p. 134.

23. "Vaccination Fact Sheet" (Monrovia, CA: National Health Federation, 1995.)

24. Kelly, 1A

25. Kelly, 4D

26. Alexander Leaf. "Preventive Medicine for Our Ailing Health Care System." *Journal of the American Medical Association* 269, no. 5 (February 3, 1993), pp. 616-618.

27. Wittels Ellison H et al. "Medical Costs of Coronary Artery Disease in the United States." *American Journal of Cardiology* 65 (February 15, 1990), pp. 432-440.

28. Leaf, pp. 616-618.

29. J Mark Sublette. "Focus on Prevention: Wellness Programs: An Untapped Resource?" *American Osteopathic Medical Association* (April-May 1991), pp. 51-53.

30. Victor Penzer. "Idealism vs the Economics and Politics of Medical Insurance." *Townsend Letter for Doctors* (August–September 1994), p. 934.

31. WDRM-FM, "Sound Off," August 19, 1991 Parker Griffith interviewed by Christopher Bird. Huntsville, AL. Transcript.

32. Ibid.

33. Statistical Abstracts of the US., U.S. Department of Commerce, Bureau of Census, U.S. Government, 1998.

34. Ibid.

35. Carl Menninger. "Changing Concepts of Disease." *Annals of Internal Medicine* 29 (July 1948), pp. 318-325.

36. Ibid.

37. Barbara Millen Posner. "Nutrition and the Global Risk for Chronic Diseases: The INTERHEALTH Nutrition Initiative." *Nutritional Reviews* 52, no. 6 (June 1994), pp. 201-207.

## Chapter 11

1. Robert O Becker. *Cross Currents*. (Los Angeles: J.P. Tarcher, 1990.) xii.

2. Thomas Kuhn T*he Structure of Scientific Revolutions*. (Chicago: University of Chicago Press, 1962.)

3. Harris Coulter. *Divided Legacy: A History of the Schism in Medical Thought* Vol. IV. (Washington, DC: Wehawken Book Co., 1995.) p. 34.

4. Ibid, p. 197.

5. Lida H Mattman. *Cell Wall Deficient Forms*. (Ann Arbor, MI: CRC Press, 1992.) p. 241.

6. Christopher Bird. *The Persecution and Trial of Gaston Naessens.* (Tiburon, CA: H.J. Kramer Inc., 1991.) p. 277.

7. William E Powles. *Human Development and Homeostasis.* (Madison, CO: International Universities Press Inc., 1992.)

8. Alastair J Cunningham. "Mind, Body, and Immune Response." *Psychoneuroimmunology*, edited by R. Ader and N. Cohen (New York: Academic Press, 1981.)

9. Sylvia Tesh. "Disease Causality and Politics." *Journal of Health Politics, Policy and Law* 6, no. 3 (Fall 1991), p. 371.

10. Beatrice Trum Hunter. "Alternative Medicine, Expanding Horizons." *Townsend Newsletter for Doctors* 144 (July 1995), p. 103.

# Selected Bibliography

## Books

Adams, F. *The Genuine Works of Hippocrates*. Baltimore, MD: Williams and Wilkins Company, 1939.

Béchamp Antoine. *Les Microzymas*. Paris: Baillier, 1883.

_____. *The Blood and Its Third Anatomical Element*. Translated by Montague R. Leverson. London: John Ousley Limited, 1912.

Becker, Robert O. *Cross Currents*. Los Angeles, CA: J.P. Tarcher, 1990.

Benison, Saul, Clifford Barger, and Elin L. Wolfe. *Walter B. Cannon – The Life and Times of a Young Scientist*. Cambridge, MA: Harvard University Press, Belknap Press, 1987.

Bernard, Claude. *An Introduction to the Study of Experimental Medicine*. (1865) Translated by H.C. Greene. New York: Dover, 1957.

_____. "Experimental Considerations Common to Living Things and Inorganic Bodies." Edited by L.L. Langley. *Homeostasis: Origin of the Concept*. Stroudburg, PA: Dowden, Hutchinson, Ross and Co., 1973.

_____. "Lessons on the Phenomena of Life Common to Animals and Vegetables." (1878) Edited by L.L. Langley. *Homeostasis: Origin of the Concept*. Stroudburg, PA: Dowden, Hutchinson, Ross and Co., 1973.

Bird, Christopher. *The Persecution and Trial of Gaston Naessens*. Tiburon, CA: H.J. Kramer Inc., 1991.

Cannon, Walter B. *The Mechanical Factors of Digestion*. London: Edward Arnold, 1891.

————. *Bodily Changes in Pain, Hunger, Fear and Rage.* New York: D. Appleton and Co., 1915.

————. *Traumatic Shock.* New York: D. Appleton and Co., 1923.

————. "Physiological Regulation of Normal States: Some Tentative Postulates Concerning Biological Homeostatics." Edited by August Pettit. *Charles Richet: Ses amis, ses collègues, ses élèves.* Paris: Les Éditions Médicales, 1926.

————. *Bodily Changes in Pain, Hunger, Fear, and Rage.* New York: D. Appleton and Co., 2nd ed., 1929.

————. "Hunger and Thirst." Edited by C. Murchison, *The Foundations of Experimental Psychology.* Worcester, MA: Clark University Press, 1929.

————. *The Wisdom of the Body.* New York: Norton, 1932. 2nd ed., 1939.

————. *The Way of an Investigator.* New York: W. W. Norton & Company Inc., 1945.

Cantwell, Alan, Jr. *AIDS and the Doctors of Death: An Inquiry Into the Origin of the AIDS Epidemic.* Los Angeles, CA: Aries Rising Press, 1988.

————. *Cancer Microbe.* Los Angeles, CA: Aries Rising Press, 1990.

Churchman, C. West. *The Systems Approach and Its Enemies.* New York: Basic Books Inc., 1979.

Coulter, Harris. *Divided Legacy: a History of the Schism in Medical Thought* Vol. IV. Washington, DC: Wehawken Book Co., 1995.

Crook, William. *The Yeast Connection.* Jackson, TN: Professional Books, 1983.

Cunningham, Alastair J. "Mind, Body, and Immune Response." *Psychoneuroimmunology.* Edited by. R. Ader and N. Cohen. New York: Academic Press, 1981.

Darwin, Charles. *Expression of the Emotions in Man and Animals.* London: John Murray, 1872.

Davidson, Alison. Compiled. *The Royal R. Rife Report.* Bayside, CA: Borderland Sciences, no date.

De Kruif, Paul. *Microbe Hunters*. New York: Harcourt, Brace and World, Inc., 1953.

Douglass, William. *Introduction to Social Psychology*. 1908.

Dubos, René. "Pasteur and Modern Science." *Pasteur Fermentation Centennial, 1847-1957*. New York: Charles Pfizer & Co. Inc., 1958.

_____. *Pasteur and Modern Science*. New York: Doubleday and Co., 1960.

_____. *Man Adapting*. New Haven, CO: Yale University Press, 1995.

_____. *Louis Pasteur – Free Lance of Science*. New York: Charles Scribner's Sons, 1976.

Duclaux, Émile. *Pasteur – The History of a Mind*. Translated by Erwin F. Smith and Florence Hedges. Philadelphia: W. B. Saunders Company, 1920.

Edwards, Sterling, and Peter Edwards. *Alex Carrel – Visionary Surgeon*. Springfield IL: Thomas Pub., 1939.

Enby, Erik, Peter Gosch, and Sheehane, Michael. *Hidden Killers: The Revolutionary Medical Discoveries of Professor Guenther Enderlein*. Sheehan Communications: 1990.

*Encyclopaedia Britannica*. New York: William Benton, 1959. s.v. "Bernard, Claude."

*Encyclopedia Americana*. Bethel, CT: Grolier Educational, 1997. s.v. "Medicine, History" and "Middle Ages, Medicine."

Enderlein, Guenther. *Bakterian Cyclogenie* [The life cycle of bacteria]. Berlin: De Gruyter, 1925.

Epstein, Samuel S. *The Politics of Cancer*. San Francisco: Sierra Club Books, 1978.

Farley, John. *The Spontaeous Generation Controversy from Descartes to Oparin*. Baltimore, MD: Johns Hopkins University Press, 1977.

Foss, Lawrence, and Kenneth Rothenberg. *The Second Medical Revolution*. Boston, MA: New Science Library, 1987.

Galdston, Imago. "Beyond the Germ Theory: The Roles of Deprivation and Stress in Health and Disease." Edited by Imago Galdston. *Beyond the Germ Theory.* New York: New York Academy of Medicine Book, 1951.

_____. *The Meaning of Social Medicine.* Cambridge, MA: Harvard University Press, 1954.

Galen (Claudius Galenus). *Galen, on the Natural Faculties.* Translated by John Brock. New York: G.P. Putnam and Sons, 1916.

Geison, Gerald L. *The Private Science of Louis Pasteur.* Princeton, NJ: Princeton University Press, 1995.

Gillespie, Charles Coulston, ed. *Dictionary of Scientific Bibliography.* New York: Charles Scribner's Sons, 1974.

Goldberg, Herbert. *Hippocrates, the Father of Medicine.* New York: F. Watts, c.1993.

Haldane, J.S. *Respiration.* New Haven, CT: Yale University Press, 1922.

Hardy, Richard H. *Homeostasis, Studies in Biology* 63. London: Edward Arnold Limited, 1982.

Hippocrates. *Great Books of the Western World – Hippocratic Writings.* Chicago: William Benton, 1952.

Holmes, Frederic L. "Origins of the Concept of the Milieu Intérieur." Edited by Francisco Grande and Maurice B. Visscher. *Claude Bernard and Experimental Medicine.* Cambridge, MA: Schenkman Publishing Company, Inc., 1967.

Hume, E. Douglas. *Béchamp or Pasteur? A Lost Chapter in the History of Biology.* Ashingdon, Rochford, Essex, England: C. W. Daniel Company Limited, 1947.

Kuhn, Thomas. *The Structure of Scientific Revolutions.* Chicago: University of Chicago Press, 1962.

Lange, Carl George, and William James. *The Emotions.* New York: Hafner Publishing, 1967.

Mattman, Lida H. *Cell Wall Deficient Forms*. Ann Arbor, MI: CRC Press, 1993.
Miller, J.G. *Living Systems*. New York: McGraw-Hill Co., 1978.

Miller, Neil Z. *Vaccines: Are They Really Safe and Effective?* Santa Fe, NM: New Atlantean Press, 1994.

Nicolle, Jacques. *Louis Pasteur – The Story of His Major Discoveries*. Philadelphia: Basic Books, Inc., 1920.

Nightingale, Florence. *Notes on Nursing*. 1859. 2nd ed. Philadelphia: J.B. Lippincott Co., 1946.

Nonclercq, Marie. *Antoine Béchamp, 1816 - 1908: L'homme et le savant, originalité et fécondité de son œuvre* [Antoine Béchamp, 1816 – 1908: The man and the scientist, the originality and the fertility of his research]. Paris: Maloine, 1982.

Olmsted, J.M.D., and I. Harris. *Claude Bernard and the Experimental Method in Medicine*. New York: Henry Schuman, 1952.

Ornish, Dean. *Dr. Dean Ornish's Program for Reversing Heart Disease*. New York: Random House, 1990.

Page, Melvin E. *Young Minds with Old Bodies*. Boston: Bruce Humphries, Inc., 1944.

_____. *Degeneration – Regeneration*. San Diego: Price Pottenger Nutritional Foundation, 1949.

_____. *Body Chemistry in Health and Disease*. St. Petersburg Beach, FL: Nutritional Development, c.1963.

Page, Melvin, and Leon H. Abrams Jr. *Health Verses Disease*. St. Petersburg Beach, FL: The Page Foundation Inc., 1960.

_____. *Your Body Is Your Best Doctor*. New Canaan, CT: Keats Publishing, 1972.

Pasteur, Louis. "The Germ Theory and Its Applications to Medicine and Surgery." Read before the French Academy of Sciences, April 29, 1878. Translated by H.C. Ernst. In *Harvard Classics* 38, pp. 364-370. New York: F.P. Collier & Sons, 1938.

_____. "The Physiological Theory of Fermentation." 1879 Translated by F. Faulkner and D.C. Robb. In *Harvard Classics* 38, pp.275-363. New York: Collier & Sons, 1938.

_____. "On the Extension of the Germ Theory." Read before the French Academy of Sciences, May 3, 1880. Translated by H.C. Ernst. In *Harvard Classics* 38, pp.371-384. New York: Collier & Sons, 1910.

_____. *Œuvres de Pasteur*. Edited by Pasteur Vallery-Radot, Seven Volumes. Paris: Masson, 1861.

_____. *Pasteur's Study on Fermentation, Harvard Case Histories in Experimental Science Case 6*. Edited by James Bryant Conant. Cambridge MA: Harvard University Press, 1952.

_____. *Pasteur's and Tyndall's Study of Spontaneous Generation, Harvard Case Histories in Experimental Science, Case 7*. Edited by James Bryant Conant. Cambridge: Harvard University Press, 1953.

Pavlov, Ivan P. *Lectures on Conditioned Reflexes. Twenty-five Years of Objective Study of the Higher Nervous Activity of Animals*. Translated from Russian by W. Horsley Gantt. New York: International Publishers Co., 1928.

Pearson, R.B. *Dream and Lie of Louis Pasteur*. P.O. Box 1767, Collingwood, Victoria, Australia: Sumeria no date.

Piel, Gerald and Osborn Segerberg Jr. eds. *The World of René Dubos – A Collection from His Writings*. New York: Henry Holt and Company, 1990.

Pouchet, Félix Archimède. *Heterogenesis: A Treatise on Spontaneous Generation*. 1859.

Powles, William E. *Human Development and Homeostasis*. Madison, CO: International Universities Press Inc., 1992.

Reich, Wilhelm. *The Cancer Biopsy*. New York: Farrar, Straus & Warren, 1973.

_____. *The Bion Experiments*. New York: Farrar, Straus & Giroux, 1979.

Richet, Charles. *Dictionnaire de Physiologie* Vol.IV. Paris: F. Alcan, 1895.

Rosenburg, Helene. *Getting Pregnant When You Thought You Couldn't*. New York: Warner Books, 1993.

Shapiro, Andrew L. *We're Number One! Where America Stands and Falls in the New World Order*. New York: Vintage, 1992.

Sharaf, Myron. *Fury on Earth – A Biography of Wilhelm Reich*. New York: St. Martin's Press/Marek, 1983.

Vallery-Radot, Pasteur. *Louis Pasteur – a Great Life in Brief*. Translated by Alfred Joseph. New York: Alfred A. Knopf, 1960.

Vallery-Radot, René. *The Life of Pasteur*. Translated by Mrs. R.L. Devonshire. New York: Doubleday, Doran, 1938.

Vandervliet, Glenn. *Microbiology and the Spontaneous Generation Debate During the 1870s*. Laurence, KA: Colorado Press, 1971.

Verner, J. R., C.W. Weiant, and R.J. Watkins. *Rational Bacteriology*. New York: H. Wolff, 1953.

von Bertalanffy, Ludwig. *General System Theory: Foundation, Developments, Applications*. New York: Braziller, 1973.

*World Health Statistics*. Geneva, Switzerland: World Health Organization, 1994.

## Journal Articles

Almquist, Ernst. "Variation and Life Cycle of Pathogenic Bacteria." *Journal of Infectious Diseases* 33 (1922): 483-493.

Aurisicchio, Louis, and C.S. Pitchumoni. "Lactose Intolerance: Recognizing the Link Between Diet and Discomfort." *Postgraduate Medicine* 95, no. 1 (January 1994): 115.

Bello, Mark. "A Look at the Prognosis and Economics of Heart Disease." *News Report* (December 1990-January 1991): 13-15.

Bernard, Claude. "Physiological Regulation of Normal States: Some Tentative Postulates Concerning Biological Homeostasis." *Selected Readings in the History of Physiology* (1926): 329-332.

Bird, Christopher. "What Has Become of the Rife Microscope?" *New Age* (March, 1976): 41-47.

_____. "The Tragedy of Innovation and Inventors Working on the Frontiers of Science." *The American Raum & Zeit* 2, no. 3. (1991), 39-46.

_____. "To Be or Not To Be." *The American Raum & Zeit* 2, no. 6. (1991): 52-59.

_____. "What the Microscope Can Reveal," *Journal of Alternative & Complementary Medicine* 10, no. 1. (January 1992): 1-12.

_____. "Seeing is Believing – Gaston Naessens and the New Biology: Part I." *Bio/Tech News*. (1993-1994, Special Issue): 1-8.

_____. "Somatids, 714-X and Curing Cancer – Gaston Naessens and the New Biology: Part II." *Bio/Tech News*. (1993-1994, Special Issue): 1-12.

Buttram, Harold E. "Overuse of Antibiotics and the Need for Alternatives." *Townsend Letter for Doctors*. (November 1991): 867-869.

Cannon, Walter B. "The Movements of the Stomach Studied by Means of the Roentgen Rays." *American Journal of Physiology* 1 (1898): 359-382.

_____. "The Movements of the Intestines Studied by Means of the Roentgen Rays." *American Journal of Physiology* 6 (1902): 251-277 and xxvii.

_____. "The Utility of Bodily Changes in Fear, Rage and Pain." *Harvard Graduates Magazine* 22 (1913-1914): 570-573.

_____. "The Emergency Function of the Adrenal Medulla in Pain and the Major Emotions." *American Journal of Physiology* 33 (1914): 356-372.

_____. "Recent Studies of Bodily Effect of Fear, Rage and Pain." *Journal of the Philosophy of Psychology and the Scientific Method* 11 (1914): 162-165.

_____. "New Evidence for Sympathetic Control of Some Internal Secretions." *American Journal of Psychiatry* 2 (1923): 15-30.

_____. "Organization for Physiological Homeostasis." *Physiological Review* 9 (1929): 399-441.

Cannon, Walter B., and R.G. Hoskins. "The Effects of Asphyxia, Hyperpnea, and Sensory Stimulation on Adrenal Secretion." *American Journal of Physiology* 29 (1911): 274-279.

Cannon, Walter B., and A. Querido. "The Role of Adrenal Secretion in the Chemical Control of Body Temperature." *Proceedings of the National Academy of Science* 10 (1924): 245-246.

Carter, K. Codell. "The Development of Pasteur's Concept of Disease Causation and the Emergence of Specific Causes in Ninetheenth-Century Medicine." *Bulletin of the History of Medicine* 65 (1989): 528-548.

Cheraskin, Emanuel. "Human Health and Homeostasis." *International Journal of Biosocial and Medical Research*. 13:1 (1991): 30.

Cheraskin, E., W.M. Ringsdorf, Jr., and A.T.S.H. Setyaadmadja et al, "The Birmingham, Alabama 1964 Diabetes Detection Drive:III Sex and Dextrostix Patterns." *Alabama Journal of Medical Science* 4 (1967): 239-291.

Christie, Celia, Mary L. Marx, Colin D. Marchant, and Shirley F. Reising. "The 1993 Epidemic of Pertussis in Cincinnati: Resurgence of Disease in a Highly Immunized Population of Children." *New England Journal of Medicine* 331, no. 1 (July 7, 1994): 16-21

Cobb, Ty. "Your Health Philosophy: The Most Important Part of Your Practice." *Townsend Letter for Doctors* (April 1995): 101-102.

Coffin, Tristam, editor. "The Health Care Crisis." *TheWashington Spectator* 14, no. 14 (August 1, 1991): 1-4.

"Colloidal Silver Offers Possible Solution to Antibiotics Crisis." *Well Mind Association of Greater Washington* (October 1995): 4-5.

Doetsch, Raymond N. "Early American Experiments on Spontaneous Generation by Jeffries Wyman (1814-1874)." *Journal of the History of Medicine and Allied Sciences* (July 1962): 325-332.

"Drugs That Cause Psychiatric Symptoms." *Medical Letter* 31, (December 29, 1989): 31.

Duclos, P., and A. Bentsi-Enchil. "Current Thoughts on the Risks and Benefits of Immunization." *Drug Safety* 8, no. 6 (1993): 404-413.

Eisenberg, D.M., R.C. Kessler, C. Foster, F.F. Norlock, D.R. Calkins, and T.L. Delbanco. "Unconventional Medicine in the United States – Prevalence, Costs, and Patterns of Use." *New England Journal of Medicine* 328. no. 4 (January 28, 1993): 246-52.

Farley, John, and Gerald L. Geison. "Science, Politics, and Spontaneous Generation in Nineteenth-century France: The Pasteur-Pouchet Debate." *Bulletin of the History of Medicine* 48, no. 2 (summer 1994): 170-182.

"Filterable Bodies Seen with the Rife Microscope." *Science – Supplement.* (December 11, 1931).

Fleming, Donald. "Walter B. Cannon and Homeostasis." Social Research 51, no. 3 (Autumn 1984): 611.

"Formula Determines Risk for NSAID–Associated Gastpathy." *Geriatrics* 45, no. 9 (September 9, 1990): 25.

Geison, Gerald L., and James A. Secord. "Pasteur and the Process of Discovery: The Case of Optical Isomerism." *Isis* 79, no. 296 (1988): 6-36.

Haldane, J.S. "Claude Bernard's Conception of the Internal Environment." *Science* 69 (1929): 432-454.

*Health Freedom News* (July/August 1992): 15-18.

Hunt, Loren, and Edward Rosenow. "Asthma-Producing Drugs." *Annals of Allergy* 68 (June 1992): 453-462.

Hunter, Beatrice Trum. "Alternative Medicine, Expanding Horizons." *Townsend Newsletter for Doctors* 144 (July 1995): 103.

"Is a New Field About to Be Opened in the Science of Bacteriology?" Editorial. *California and Western Medicine* 36, no. 6 (December, 1931): 461.

Jackson, Bob. "Melvin E. Page, D.D.S. – The Story of a Nutritional Pioneer – 1894-1983." *Price-Pottenger Nutrition Foundation Health Journal* 19, no. 4 (Winter 1995): 7-9.

Kalenbach, Jane C. "Endocrine Aspects of Homeostasis." *American Zoology* 28, 761-773.

Kalokerinos A., and G.C. Dettman. "Second Thoughts About Disease – A Controversy and Béchamp Revisited." *Journal of the International Academy of Preventive Medicine* IV, no. 1 (July, 1977): 4-24.

Kelly, Dennis. "Many Elderly Given Inappropriate Drugs." *USA Today* (August 8, 1995): IA.

Kenton, Leslie. "What the Microscope Can Reveal." *International Journal of Alternative and Complementary Medicine* 10, no. 1 (January, 1992): 11-12.

Klotter, Julie. "Floxin." *Townsend Newsletter for Doctors* 143 (June 1995): 11.

Leaf, Alexander. "Preventive Medicine for Our Ailing Health Care System." *Journal of the American Medical Association* 269, no. 5 (February 3, 1993): 616-618.

Lemer, Patricia and Kelly Dorfman. "Survey Shows Link Between Antibiotics and Developmental Delays in Children." *Townsend Newsletter for Doctors* (October 1995): 9.

Menninger, Carl. "Changing Concepts of Disease." *Annals of Internal Medicine* 29 (July 1948): 318-325.

*Morbidity and Mortality Weekly Report* 46 (October 30, 1997): 1013-1026.

Olarsch, Gerald, and Susan Stockton. "Why Are Kids Killing Kids?" *Sarasota Eco Report* 5, no. 10 (October 1995): 1.

Pasteur, Louis. "Louis Pasteur's Credo of Science: His Address When He Was Inducted into the French Academy." Translated by Eli Moschocwitz. *Bulletin of the History of Medicine* 22 (1989): 528-548.

Penzer, Victor. "Idealism vs the Economics and Politics of Medical Insurance." *Townsend Letter for Doctors* (August-September 1994): 934.

Pinner, Robert W., Steven M. Teutsch, Lone Simonsen, Laura Klug, Judith M. Graber, Matthew J. Clarke, and Ruth L. Berkelman. "Trends in Infectious Diseases Mortality in the United States," *Journal of the American Medical Association*, vol. 275, no. 3 (1996), pp. 189-93.

Posner, Barbara Millen. "Nutrition and the Global Risk for Chronic Diseases: The INTERHEALTH Nutrition Initiative." *Nutrition Reviews* 52, no. 6 (June 1994): 201-207.

Rife, Royal Raymond, and Arthur Isaac Kendall. "Observations on Bacillus Typhosus in Its Filterable State." *California and Western Medicine* xxxv, no. 6 (December 1931): 109-111.

"Rife's Microscope." *The Smithsonian Report*. Annual Report of the Board of Regents of the Smithsonian Institution (1944).

Roll-Hansen, Nils. "Experimental Method and Spontaneous Generation: The Controversy between Pasteur and Pouchet, 1859-64." *Journal of the History of Medicine* (July, 1979): 273-292.

Rosenow, Edward C. "Transmutations Within the Streptococcus-Pneumococcus Group." *Journal of Infectious Diseases* 14 (January 1914): 1-31.

Russell, Christine. "Louis Pasteur and Questions of Fraud." *Townsend Letter for Doctors* (October 1993): 960.

Seguin, C. Alberto. "The Concept of Disease." *Psychosomatic Medicine* 8 (1946): 252-253.

Stratton, K.R., C.J. Howe, and R.B. Johnston Jr. "Adverse Events Associated with Childhood Vaccines: Evidence Bearing on Causality." *Journal of the American Medical Association* 271, no. 20 (May 25, 1994): 1602-1905.

Sublette, J. Mark. "Focus on Prevention: Wellness Programs: An Untapped Resource?" *American Osteopathic Medical Association* (April-May 1991): 51-53.

Sullivan, M.D. "Reconsidering the Wisdom of the Body: An Epistemological Critique of Claude Bernard's Concept of the Internal Environment." *Journal of Medicine and Philosophy* 15, no. 5 (October 1990): 493-514.

Tesh, Sylvia. "Disease Causality and Politics." *Journal of Health Politics, Policy and Law* 6, no. 3 (Fall 1991): 369-391.

Veatch, R. "Voluntary Risks to Health: The Ethical Issue." *Journal of the American Medical Association* 243 (January 4, 1980): 50-55.

Williams, R.D., "Nature, Nurture and Family Predisposition." *New England Journal of Medicine*, 318 (1988): 7691-7692.

Wittels, Ellison H. "Medical Costs of Coronary Artery Disease in the United States." *American Journal of Cardiology* 65 (February 15, 1990): 432-440.

Wolfe, Sidney M. "Adverse Drug Reactions: Why Do They Occur and How Serious Is the Problem?" *Health Letter* 10 (October 1993): 1-3, 6.

## Government Publications

*U.S.Industrial Outlook 1994*, Commerce Department of the U.S. Government. pp.74-75.

*Historical Statistics of U.S. – Colonial Times to 1970.* Superintendent of Documents, U.S. Government Printing Office, 1975.

*Statistical Abstracts of the U.S.* Superintendent of Documents, U.S. Government Printing Office, 1993.

*Statistical Abstracts of the U.S.* 114. U.S. Bureau of Census, 1994.

*U.S. Government on Health and Human Services.* National Center for Health Statistics, 1994.

## Unpublished Papers

Aisenberg, Andrew Robert. "Contagious Disease and the Government of Paris in the Age of Pasteur." Ph.D. dissertation, Yale University, 1993.

Béchamp, Antoine. "Nutrition." Conference at Lyon, France for the Montpellier Medical Society. August, 1868. Dossier Lectures. Paris: Library of the Academy of Science.

_____. Communication to the Academy of Medicine. May 3, 1870. Dossier Letters. Paris: Library of the Academy of Science.

_____. Letters to Senator J.B. Dumas. Dossier Dumas. Library of the Academy of Science, Paris.

Bird, Christopher. "The Mystery of Pleomorphic (Form-Changing) Microbial Organisms: One Brief Overview." Paper presented at "Symposium 1991: From Béchamp's Microzyma to the Somatid Theory: Somatidian Orthobiology," June 8-9, 1991, at Centre d'Orthobiologie Somatidienne Inc., Sherbrooke, Quebec, Canada.

Cannon, Walter B. Letter to Cornelia J. Cannon. December 24 and December 26, 1905. Cannon Papers, Countway Medical Library, Harvard University, Boston, MA.

"Vaccination Fact Sheet." Monrovia, CA: National Health Federation, 1995.

WDRM-FM, Huntsville, AL. "Sound Off." August 19, 1991. Parker Griffith interviewed by Christopher Bird. Transcript.

# AUDIO CASSETTE TAPES

The following audio cassette tapes present information on a variety of subjects. An order form is provided on the following page.

**Lick the Sugar Habit** – An introduction the the book, this tapes provides detailed explanations of the body chemistry principle, mineral relationships, the endocrine system enzymes, and promoters of infectious and degenerative disease. (1 hour)

**Allergies** – What are food allergies? What causes them? How can they be eliminated? Learn how foods to which you have an allergic reaction can be reintroduced in your diet. Environmental allergies are also discussed. (1 hour).

**Osteoporosis** – Although you may be getting a reasonable amount of calcium in your diet, if your body chemistry is upset, the calcium cannot be absorbed properly. This tape explains how to look for symptoms of calcium deficiency and how to test for susceptibility to osteoporosis. (1 hour)

**Obesity** – The latest research on the relationship of allergies, addictions, and cravings to obesity is presented. (30 minutes) **Women** is on the other side.

**Women** – Information on premenstrual syndrome (PMS), candidiasis (yeast infections), menstruation, menopause, and postmenopausal problems is provided. (30 minutes) **Obesity** is on the other side.

**Children** – This tape begins with a discussion on prenatal nutrition. Information of food allergies and eating problems for infants and children follows. Ideas for encouraging older children and teenagers to eat nutritious foods end the tape. (1 hour)

**Food Preparation** – This tape answers the following questions: Where can I shop for the best, most nutritious foods? How can I best prepare food to keep it from upsetting the body's chemical balance? What should I know about food additives, irradiation, insecticides, and fungicides? (1 hour)

**Urine and pH Testing** – Information and instructions for testing homeostasis through saliva and urine are presented. Common causes of upset body chemistry are discussed, as well as ways to regain the body's chemical balance. (1 hour)

**New Information** – Medical research will be given which shows the relationship of nutrition to disease. Some of the subjects discussed are milk products, fluoride, rancid, over processed, over heated and hydrogenated fats, and other data. (1 hour)

**Our Diet - Our Immune System** – Listen to a lecture given by Nancy Appleton, Ph.D., explaining more about health, disease, homeostasis and body chemistry. The last fifteen minutes are devoted to helpful questions from the audience and answers. (1.5 hours)

# AUDIO CASSETTE
## Order Form

Name: _____

Address:_____ Apt.: _____

City:_____

State: _____ Zip:_____

List Cassette Titles:

1. _____  5. _____

2. _____  6. _____

3. _____  7. _____

4. _____  8. _____

9. _____

*Price List

| Quantity | Price | Shipping | Shipping to Canada (U.S. currency) |
|---|---|---|---|
| 1 | $ 6.50 | $1.25 | $1.50 |
| 2 | $12.00 | $1.50 | $1.75 |
| 3 | $15.00 | $1.75 | $2.00 |
| 4 | $20.00 | $2.00 | $2.25 |
| 5 | $25.00 | $2.25 | $2.50 |
| 6 | $30.00 | $2.50 | $2.75 |
| 7 | $35.00 | $2.75 | $3.00 |
| 8 | $40.00 | $3.00 | $3.25 |
| 9 | $45.00 | $3.25 | $3.50 |

**California Residents Only,** please apply appropriate sales tax or 10%.

Mail this completed form, along with a check made payable to Nancy Appleton, Ph.D., to

Nancy Appleton, Ph.D.
P.O. Box 3083
Santa Monica CA 90403

# BODY CHEMISTRY TEST KIT
## Order Form

This kit contains tests that determine if your body chemistry is in homeostasis, in balance. Solution for 250 tests, two test tubes, and eye-dropper, a brush for cleaning the test tubes and pH paper for testing the acid/alkalinity of the urine and saliva are included. An informative 28-page booklet, *Monitoring Your Basic Health*, which contains information on body chemistry—what upsets it and how to regain and maintain its balance—is also included. The booklet also provides suggested food plans and instructions on how to test for food allergies. The two accompanying one-hour audio cassette tapes, "How Our Diet Affects Our Immune System" and "pH and Urine Testing," will give you a further understanding of homeostasis and of the testing process.

Name: _____

Address:_____ Apt.: _____

City:_____

State: _____ Zip:_____

Cost of Body Chemistry Test Kit*
1 kit                                              $30.00
Shipping                                       $ 3.50
Shipping to Canada (U.S. currency)    $ 4.00

**California residents only,** please add appropriate sales tax or 10%.

Mail this completed form, along with a check made payable to Nancy Appleton, Ph.D.

Nancy Appleton, Ph.D.
P.O. Box 3083
Santa Monica CA 90403

e-mail: riters@ix.netcom.com
web-site: www.nancyappleton.com

# About the Author

Nancy Appleton earned her BS in clinical nutrition from U.C.L.A. and her Ph.D. from Walden University in health services. She maintains a private practice in Santa Monica, California. An avid researcher, Dr. Appleton lectures extensively throughout the world and has appeared on numerous television and radio talk shows. In addition to *The Curse of Louis Pasteur*, she is author of the best selling *Lick the Sugar Habit*, *Secrets of Natural Healing with Food*, and *Healthy Bones*.

# Index

## Other Books by Nancy Appleton, PhD

**LICK THE SUGAR HABIT** - We are a nation of sugarholics, consuming, on the average, over 150 pounds of sugar and sweeteners a year. *Lick the Sugar Habit* shows how sugar upsets the body chemistry and devastates the endocrine and immune systems, leading to a host of diseases and conditions including hypoglycemia, diabetes, osteoporosis, arthritis, cancer, heart disease, headaches, allergies, asthma, obesity, periodontal disease, tooth decay, and more. A sugarholic since childhood, Dr. Appleton cured herself of chronic illnesses including bronchitis and pneumonia by changing her lifestyle. She has a self-help program to help you lick the sugar habit and live a healthier life. Food plans and recipes to help you on your way are included.

**HEALTHY BONES** - Osteoporosis is a weakening of the bone structure that results in a slow, insidious loss of calcium. It is a degenerative disease that starts slowly - for some in childhood and for others in adulthood. Dr. Appleton has uncovered a way to prevent osteoporosis without costly drugs, extensive supplements, and expensive treatments. Her theory is remarkably simple. Instead of treating the symptom - a loss of calcium - she looks at the cause - why calcium is drawn from the bones in the first place. By understanding the principle of body chemistry balance, Dr. Appleton shows us what we do to bring on calcium loss and what we can do to correct the problem, written in easy-to-understand language. Included are food plans and delicious recipes to help the reader follow the program.

**THE SECRETS OF NATURAL HEALING WITH FOOD** - Here is a definitive book about achieving homeostasis, balanced body chemistry. This book addresses the impact of diet, food allergies, and environmental contaminants on the body and explores in detail the mind-body connection, osteoporosis, arthritis, diabetes, hypoglycemia, PMS, and Candida Albicans. Dr. Appleton provides a comprehensive, inspiring program which includes food plans, recipes, charts, graphs, and self-assessment exercises to strengthen your immune system and lead you to your optimal state of health.